1841 *$12.99*

W9-BPN-190

When the Cradle Is Empty

John and Sylvia Van Regenmorter

Marion Powell
Women's Health Information Centre

TYNDALE

Tyndale House Publishers, Inc.
Wheaton, Illinois

WHEN THE CRADLE IS EMPTY

Library of Congress Cataloging-in-Publication Data
Van Regenmorter, John.
   When the cradle is empty : answering tough questions about infertility / John and
Sylvia Van Regenmorter.—1st ed.
      p. cm. — (Focus on the family)
Includes bibliographical references.
   ISBN 1-58997-157-4
   1. Infertility. 2. Infertility—Psychological aspects. I. Van Regenmorter, Sylvia. II. Title.
III. Focus on the Family presents.
RC889 .V243 2004
   618.1'78—dc22

                                        2003017445

A Focus on the Family book published by Tyndale House Publishers, Wheaton, Illinois.

Focus on the Family books are available at special quantity discounts when purchased in
bulk by corporations, organizations, churches, or groups. Special imprints, messages, and
excerpts can be produced to meet your needs. For more information, contact: Focus on the
Family Sales Department, 8605 Explorer Drive, Colorado Springs, CO 80920; or phone
(800) 932-9123.

Editor: John Duckworth
Cover design and photo: Mark Waters

Printed in the United States of America

04 05 06 07 08 09 10/10 9 8 7 6 5 4 3 2 1

Contents

∞

Thanks to . . .

Mary Ann Boyer
Glenn De Mots
William G. Dodds, M.D.
Joe S. McIlhaney, Jr., M.D.
Martheen Versluys

Whether you offered practical assistance or words of encouragement, your help has been deeply appreciated—particularly in the early stages of writing this book, when completing the manuscript and finding a publisher were distant dreams. You blessed us with your support.

Thanks also to John Duckworth, Stacey Herebic, and the other gifted folks at Focus on the Family. You took our rough-hewn manuscript and made us look better than we deserve.

Thanks as well to the named and unnamed individuals whose stories of hurt, hope, and faith are found within these pages. We couldn't have written this book without you!

Above all, thanks to our gracious Savior. Though we sometimes wondered if He was walking with us on the journey of infertility, we now realize that He was there every step of the way. In gratitude we dedicate this book to Him, and our prayer is that He will use it to help many others who are still on the way.

There Is an Empty Room

There is an empty room
In which no child sleeps;
Just a rocking chair, a teddy bear,
The baby clothes they keep.
It is a quiet room
With everything in place;
But no happy sighs or lullabies,
No child in their embrace.
There is an empty crib
In the corner, tucked away;
The gentle light of the moon shines bright
As they kneel by the crib to pray . . .
"Remove all bitter thoughts,
Your will is what we seek.
Dry our tears and calm our fears,
Lift us up, for we are weak."

There is an empty room
In which no child sleeps.
But they know the love of a Father above,
And His promises He keeps.[1]

Introduction

∞

For whom is this book written?
- Married couples who are finding it difficult to have a baby;
- Spouses who discover that infertility is straining their marriage;
- Believers who find that childlessness is weakening their faith;
- Couples puzzled by all the options for treating infertility;
- Those who seek to encourage their spouses who are disappointed over a failure to conceive;
- Couples who grieve the children they've lost in miscarriage or at birth;
- Those considering adoption; and
- Family members, pastors, counselors, and others who want to understand those whose cradles are empty.

By whom is this book written?

To understand that, you need to know a little of our story.

Married in John's last year of seminary, we struggled with infertility for almost six years before adopting our first child, John Mark. Knowing there was room in our hearts and home for more children, we continued medical treatment for infertility, including two surgeries for Sylvia. Finally, believing God's plan for us didn't include biological parenting, we adopted a daughter, Sarah, in 1982.

Feeling doubly blessed, we were content with our family of four. After discontinuing all medical treatment, we became deeply involved in ministry to infertile couples. John completed a Doctor of Ministry degree, and Sylvia helped to start a RESOLVE support group for infertile couples in Sioux Falls, South Dakota.

God, meanwhile, had a surprise for us. At the ripe old age of 38 (Sylvia) and 39 (John), we were suddenly expecting! We were also dumbfounded, to say the least. Now we're triply blessed; our daughter Rebecca is an added joy.

We never would have chosen the journey of infertility. But we're grateful that God has used this journey to make us stronger and more mature in our faith. We're more conscious of our dependence on Him, more certain of His love, more grateful for every blessing, and more eager to serve Him in ministry to others.

When we discovered that we might not have biological children, we experienced questions, including, "Why, God?"

We experienced loneliness. Why did everyone around us seem to have children?

We experienced well-meaning but ignorant advice: "Why don't you just adopt and you'll get pregnant?"

We experienced doubts. Was infertility a curse?

We visited half a dozen physicians, spent thousands of dollars, and saw moments of great expectation crushed by agonizing failure.

Through these experiences two things occurred.

First, we learned. We did so slowly and sometimes painfully, but we learned. We learned that it's important to seek the most qualified physician available. We learned that high-tech infertility treatment can involve difficult ethical dilemmas. We learned that unintended hurts come from loving but uninformed friends. We learned how to challenge the spiritual doubts that plague many Christians who experience infertility.

Secondly, we gained the desire to help fellow travelers on this journey. As a result we've spent over 15 years in ministry to fellow infertile couples, including those who've experienced pregnancy loss. That ministry began when we co-authored a book with Dr. Joe S. McIlhaney called *Dear God, Why Can't We Have a Baby?* (Baker Book House, 1986).

Our ministry took a giant leap forward in 1996 when we became editors of *Stepping Stones*, a newsletter devoted to providing information and encouragement for those struggling with fertility issues. Today *Stepping Stones* is a ministry of Bethany Christian Services, a national and international Christian adoption and family services agency. The *Stepping Stones* newsletter is distributed to thousands of couples around the world.

Some have said to us, "You have two children through adoption and one through birth. What more do you want? Why are you still involved in this infertility work?"

We're not involved because there's something we want. It's because we have something to give.

The best of what we've learned is now available in the book you hold. It's a privilege to share what we've learned with you!

1

A Journey Begins

by Sylvia

∞

Many metaphors can be used to picture the problem of infertility. It can be described as a roller coaster or a nightmare, for example—or, as one person put it, "a rushing stream preventing me from crossing over into the land of parenthood."

When it comes to infertility, the metaphor I like best is "journey."

I like it because a journey has a beginning and an end. It's purposeful, not pointless. It implies activity, not passivity.

Infertility is an emotional journey; before you've completed it, you'll experience all the emotions known to humankind.

STEP 1: THE FOG

The journey begins in a haze. Perhaps you've been married for several years and no children have come. You may have used "the pill" for a year or two while you settled into married life and built up a savings account. But you've been off birth control for some time and nothing has happened.

Perhaps you assumed that pregnancy would come easily because your sister is a "fertile Myrtle" who had three children in five years. Maybe the story of this wife who wrote to us sounds familiar:

> I know that you have probably heard my story a million times. We began our marriage, as the song says, with "bright hopes and promises." We had it all figured out. George and I were married when we were 23 years old, and we decided that we would have our first child when we turned 26. After trying to become pregnant for over a year, we wonder if the Lord has different plans.

In the back of your mind you begin to wonder why you haven't become pregnant, but probably feel no real worry. You think that if you and your spouse were able to get away for a few weekends, or if you felt rested enough to make love more often . . .

For others on this beginning leg of the journey, getting pregnant isn't the problem. You conceive and celebrate. You can't wait to tell your mother and your best friends; you begin making plans. Then suddenly there's a cramp, a patch of red, a frantic call to the doctor. Before you know it, your pregnancy has ended. Your disappointment is huge. You bristle at the comments of those who belittle your loss. Still, you tell yourself that you and your spouse will try again, and next time . . .

STEP 2: THE REALIZATION

You continue in the fog until slowly, gradually, it dawns on you that something is wrong. You should have become pregnant by now. Each month you hope for the best, but each month you're disappointed again.

When asked about starting your family, you may laugh it off. "Why get tied down so early?" you say. "We're going to enjoy life a little first."

But inwardly you're becoming disturbed: *What's wrong? All our friends are getting pregnant; why can't we?*

Or perhaps you have another miscarriage. Like this wife, you lose your baby once more: "Soon I was pregnant, but we lost our baby at only eight weeks. We were deeply disappointed, but we knew God would provide. Six months later, I was pregnant again, and again I miscarried."

STEP 3: DOWNPLAYING THE PROBLEM

In some ways, the next part of the journey is the easiest. The fog is lifting; you're ready to acknowledge that you have a problem. But you assume the infertility specialist you've selected can help you. As one wife recalls, "After two years of trying to get pregnant, we decided to work with an infertility specialist. He discovered that I had too many antibodies in my system but he was confident we could work around them."

At this stage many couples think, "It's something minor, right?" In your eyes, infertility is merely a slight detour in your plans. The burden on your back isn't heavy. You see no need to pack a suitcase for this journey; an overnight bag will be enough.

STEP 4: THE SHOCK

Suddenly you fall off a cliff, hitting the bottom with a startled thud. Your physician has discovered that there's something seriously wrong with you—or your spouse.

"Doctor," you say, "you've got to be kidding!" But she isn't. You may feel like the woman who told us, "Our doctor has informed us that I have stage four endometriosis—which is the most advanced stage you can get."

Shock is usually the shortest stop on the journey. Soon you'll climb back up the cliff. Though you are shaken, you are unbowed.

Step 5: Denial and Anger

With renewed energy and determination you plunge down the path—blindly. You charge ahead, oblivious to roadblocks. Though you may not realize it, you're in denial.

Convinced that the diagnosis is wrong, you tell yourself, "There must be some mistake. I want that test redone." Perhaps your denial takes a spiritual turn: "God is just testing us. Surely He'll let us have a successful pregnancy soon!"

Denial can swiftly veer into the thorns and thistles of anger. You may become angry with your physician: "He is so insensitive, so incompetent, so expensive."

Your anger may turn against your spouse: "Why can't you come with me to the next doctor's appointment? I always go alone!"

You may become angry with yourself: "It's stupid to get so upset about this problem," you might say, or, "I hate being so jealous of my sister and her children."

You may get mad at God, as one woman admitted to us: "I'm kind of angry with God right now. Why does He give me the desire to have a baby, and then not allow me to fulfill that desire?"

Step 6: Guilt and Depression

Anger doesn't usually last long. Before you realize it, you're slipping down into the valley of guilt: "If only I hadn't used birth control"; "If only I'd had more self-control when we were dating"; "If only I'd gone to the doctor sooner"; "If only I'd been a better Christian." Much of the guilt may be unrealistic, but at the time you don't recognize it.

You begin to hate it when your friends happily announce that they're pregnant. You make excuses for not attending baby showers, but that makes you feel terribly guilty; after all, doesn't the Bible say to "rejoice with those who rejoice"? Maybe you feel like the would-be mom who said, "I was genuinely thrilled for my friend, but I honestly did not want to attend the shower. I knew I would hate it. At the same time, I was angry at myself for feeling this way."

At the bottom of the valley you encounter depression. This can take many forms; you may simply feel dragged out or unattractive, or you may lose all desire for sex and stop caring about your personal appearance.

STEP 7: WEARINESS

It's difficult to leave depression completely behind. You may fall into it again periodically, but in the meantime you continue the journey. You discover that the trip is much longer than you'd first thought. Instead of taking a short walk, you're heading down a road that stretches for miles.

The sun is hot now as you trudge the dusty path. You're getting weary. You pray, but you're tired of praying because no one seems to answer. When you share your burden with others, they respond with platitudes. As one worn-out traveler put it, "If I hear someone tell me one more time to 'just relax and it will happen,' I'm going to explode!"

You endure tests and more tests, and still no end is in sight.

WHERE DOES THE JOURNEY END?

Each couple's pathway through infertility is unique. Yours may not include all of the aforementioned steps. But the chances are that you find yourself at some point along that itinerary.

Maybe you're at the beginning of the journey. Your burden is light, your hopes are high, and the road doesn't seem too steep or long. Indeed, your journey may well end in a successful pregnancy. That's the experience of two-thirds of those who undergo treatment for infertility. Even if you stop medical treatment, you may be surprised as this letter-writer was: "After struggling for many years with unexplained infertility, God blessed us with a wonderfully healthy son. What a joy it was for us to celebrate our tenth anniversary."

Or perhaps you've been on this trek longer than you care to remember. There are no "surprises" in sight. The road keeps stretching endlessly into the horizon, and you wonder, "How and when will this end?"

Your journey will end in its own day and in its own way. I don't know where yours will take you, but I do know this: Through faith in God, your journey will end with joy, not despair; with hope, rather than doubt; with fullness in the place of emptiness.

I hope and pray that this book will help you on your way!

"For I know the plans I have for you," declares the LORD, "plans to prosper you and not to harm you, plans to give you hope and a future." (Jeremiah 29:11)

2

Pitfalls Along
the Path

by John and Sylvia

> "Ve are too soon alt
> und too late schmart."

This Yankee-German phrase expresses exactly how we dealt with our infertility—at least in the early stages. We were indeed too soon old and too late smart! We blundered into several pitfalls that cost us dearly.

We want to describe some of those hazards in the hope that you'll avoid them.

TAKING GOD FOR GRANTED

"If it is thy will, grant them the laughter of little children." This was part of a prayer during our wedding ceremony as we set out on the adventure of marriage, full of hope and energy. Little did we realize the number of prayers that would be said and tears that would be shed before we were granted that request.

Looking back, we're surprised that we assumed all married couples have children. Both of us came from large families, yet each of us had relatives or friends who were never able to conceive. Knowing several childless couples should have given us a clue that marriage doesn't come with a "Have the child of your dreams or double your money back" guarantee. Somehow we presumed an inalienable right to be parents. In fact, a few months after our marriage we'd already chosen the names of our children: John Mark and Sarah.

We've come to learn that many couples today are the same way. As a pastor, John meets with prospective spouses for several premarital counseling sessions before he officiates at their wedding. At some point they discuss the subject of children. John asks the starry-eyed young couple, "Do you hope to have children someday?"

Inevitably the bride-to-be will smile sweetly, glance at her fiancé, and blurt out something like, "Oh, yes! Michael and I have discussed this a lot, haven't we, Michael? We've decided I should keep working for at least two years so we can save money—right, Michael? Then when we're ready, we'll have at least two kids—hopefully at least three years apart. But we do want them close enough together to be friends, isn't that right, Michael? We're hoping to have a boy and a girl because I just really want a little girl since I never had a baby sister, and I know Michael really wants a boy, don't you, Michael? By the way, Pastor, I just know Michael will make a really great dad. I can picture him taking our son fishing, and playing ball in the backyard. So we're going to have at least one girl and one boy."

That might be a bit of a caricature, but not much! A majority of young couples take children for granted.

In the biblical age it was different. Solomon, the writer of Psalm 127, was profoundly aware that God controls human lives and fortunes, including one's fertility:

> Unless the LORD builds the house,
>   its builders labor in vain.
> Unless the LORD watches over the city,
>   the watchmen stand guard in vain.
> In vain you rise early
>   and stay up late,
> toiling for food to eat—
>   for he grants sleep to those he loves.
> Sons are a heritage from the LORD,
>   children a reward from him.
>
> Psalm 127:1-3

There was a realization in those days that children are a gift from God—a gift that depends on His timetable, not ours. They are a gift that requires His blessing, not human will. In our age we have lost some of this humbling awareness of our dependence on God.

FACING UP TO THE PROBLEM

Since we assumed we would have children, we were tenaciously reluctant to admit we might have a problem. It was well over two years after we began trying to have a baby that we became serious about seeking medical help.

Ironically, we considered adopting a child before we tried to conceive one. About six months after our wedding, during an internship in the Philippines, we felt the desire to adopt a child from that economically challenged nation. But we decided to have our biological children first;

maybe later we would adopt one of the Filipino youngsters who tugged on our heartstrings.

Returning from the Philippines, we were anxious to begin our family. Friends and relatives obviously were waiting for the same event, since we were frequently asked, "Are you pregnant yet?" We said no, but were sure it wouldn't be long before we could respond with an excited yes.

Months passed without a pregnancy, but we weren't alarmed. Surely the delay was due to the pressures of recent moves and the challenges of our new ministry in New Jersey. Even when a year went by and "we" didn't become pregnant, the issue was no more than a pinprick in the back of our minds. We didn't worry, panic, or dwell on our concerns. We stayed confident that in due time God would grace our marriage with children.

Looking back on our laid-back attitude, we realize that we squandered crucial time by not pursuing medical treatment aggressively after that first year. Second-guessing is easy, of course—and before we were through with our infertility journey we would do plenty of it.

Many couples let three, four, or even five years slip by before they squarely face the fact that they have a problem. Letting that much time pass without seeking medical treatment is a serious mistake.

WHY THE WAIT?

The reasons why couples put off seeking treatment for infertility vary. Often they believe their inability to achieve a successful pregnancy is due to something insignificant—something that, given time, they can overcome by themselves. Perhaps, they think, they don't make love often enough—or too often. Maybe the wife is run down and needs vitamins; perhaps they haven't quite mastered the right technique of intercourse. Surely next month, or the next time they make love, it will happen.

Others find it demeaning to admit to an infertility problem, thinking it suggests inadequacy or a humiliating flaw. Even the term *infertil-*

ity can be a stumbling block. One friend of ours has been trying to achieve a pregnancy for at least two years, but steadfastly refuses to use the term *infertile*. "I am not infertile," she insists. In her mind, "infertile" means "sterile."

When should a couple face the problem and begin seeking medical help? If you've been trying and failing for a year or more to achieve a successful pregnancy, it's not too early to be concerned and to seek out an infertility specialist. This rule of thumb stems from the generally accepted definition of infertility—which is the inability to become pregnant after a year or more of regular sexual relations without contraception, or the inability to carry a pregnancy to a live birth. Don't be dissuaded by family, friends, or even a spouse, who may encourage you to hang on and give it more time. Remember, those around us can be just as prone to denial as we are!

"IT'S HER, NOT HIM, RIGHT?"

Another mistake we made is a common one: unconsciously assuming that infertility stems from the female half of the marriage.

Picture this scene from those days: We're sitting in our living room, and once more the conversation turns to the fact that Sylvia isn't getting pregnant. For the umpteenth time we rehash all the questions, frustrations, and intercessions that have come to dominate our lives.

Finally John senses that he needs to exercise some leadership. "Okay, honey," he says firmly. "We have talked about this enough; I think it's time for some action. Tomorrow morning I want you to call the doctor and go in for a checkup."

Sylvia agrees. The next morning she calls a physician, and the following week she goes in for an initial appointment—alone.

Despite statistics indicating that 45 percent of all infertility is due to a male factor, many couples assume the trouble stems from the female side of the marriage. In most cases, it's the wife who makes the initial contact with the physician; she's the one who goes to the first appointment, often by herself; and she's the one who undergoes the first battery of tests.

Why presume that the medical problem originates in the woman? Unless a complete infertility workup is done on both partners, the full picture of the problem may not be revealed.

CHOOSING DR. WRONG

When we finally realized that we needed medical care, we were not selective enough in choosing a physician. We went to an obstetrician/gynecologist who advertised infertility as one of his specialties. Unfortunately, his other specialty was prenatal care and delivering babies. This meant that each time we went for an appointment, we had to sit in a waiting room with pregnant women.

One day Sylvia overheard the conversation of two other women who were also waiting to see the doctor. One was 37; the other looked 18 at most.

The younger one asked the older if she was happy with her pregnancy. "Oh, yes," the older one replied. "But I'll be glad when it's over; I just hope we have a boy. I've had five girls, and my husband wants a boy. He'll kill me if it's a girl."

The younger one declared that she hoped she wasn't pregnant. "I'm too young to have a baby," she said matter-of-factly. "Of course, if I am pregnant, I'll get an abortion. There's no way I'm taking care of a kid!"

As Sylvia hid behind her magazine and pretended not to listen, her ears were stinging and her eyes were wet. Hard questions raged through her mind: "Dear God, why are You giving a sixth child to a family that already has five—and they're fussy about gender to boot? Why didn't You make me pregnant instead of this immature teenager? Then Your world could be spared another abortion."

Thankfully, Sylvia was soon called in to see the doctor. Her questions were forgotten—for the moment.

This doctor had the reputation of being a fine physician and a warm human being. In many respects he was probably the former, and we certainly did experience the latter. But he definitely was not the best choice for infertility treatment.

Too late, we discovered that our physician had not received the most advanced training for infertility. Had we done our homework, we would have realized that he was not practicing state-of-the-art medical care.

We allowed this physician to do surgery on Sylvia—an unwise decision because each surgery, even a laparoscopy, may have complications that, in some cases, may hinder the ability to conceive. If surgery is needed, it's important to have a physician who will do it right the first time.

In the years following, we've talked to numerous couples who have spent time, energy, and money on medical care that is simply not the best available. Too often the story goes something like this:

> When we first suspected that we might have a problem, I went to the Yellow Pages and looked up the list of ob/gyns who advertised that they did infertility work. I found a Dr. Smith there who advertised that he could provide care for "Surgery—Pregnancy—Infertility—Menopause—Pap Smears—Pelvic Pain." I thought to myself, "Aha! Dr. Smith can do it all. And he is conveniently located." So I went for an initial appointment, and he really is nice! I have been going to him for the last two years, and I really think the world of him as a person. Unfortunately, we have not become pregnant.
>
> Lately I have done some reading, and I am not sure that Dr. Smith is the most qualified physician available. Through my reading and conversations with friends, I have come to realize that Dr. Jones, a board-certified reproductive endocrinologist, is probably the best infertility specialist in our area. In addition, Dr. Jones has his

own lab and does not need to send out specimens to a generic lab to be tested. Dr. Jones is also qualified in providing hi-tech treatments if we decide to go that route.

When I have suggested to Dr. Smith that maybe it is time for a second opinion with Dr. Jones, he seems threatened and informs me that he can perform all the tests as well as Dr. Jones can. I just don't know what to do. I don't want to hurt Dr. Smith, but I feel I would get better medical care with Dr. Jones.

CHOOSING DR. RIGHT

Because choosing a physician is critical, we encourage you to consider the following suggestions.

1. Don't assume that every ob/gyn is interested or skilled in treating infertility. Ask the doctor how much infertility work he or she does. You can waste precious time and energy, not to mention expense, in seeing a physician who merely dabbles in infertility treatment. It would be nice if such doctors would routinely refer patients to those who are more specialized, but that doesn't always happen. Physicians are human, and for some it's a blow to the ego to admit that they can't help a patient. As Dr. Joe S. McIlhaney puts it, "Many physicians are not really interested in fertility but do not want to have their patients go to another physician."[1]

2. If possible, find a physician who is board-certified in reproductive endocrinology. Dr. Jeffrey A. Keenan puts it bluntly:

Many couples still are not aware that there is generally a very substantial difference between being treated by a general obstetrician/gynecologist and a reproductive endocrinologist. The general gynecologist typically receives only four to six weeks of training in infertility during his or her residency. Following this, they typically may see one or two infertility patients each week.

This is in stark contrast to the reproductive endocrinologist, who has an additional two to three years of infertility training and research experience following residency. Most of these physicians then specialize in infertility care, with 60 percent to 90 percent of their patients being seen for such treatment. This often translates into a more efficient, less expensive evaluation and more successful outcome.[2]

In fairness, it must be said that there are many ob/gyns who, though not board-certified reproductive endocrinologists, have taken advantage of advanced training and workshops in infertility and are very competent to begin an infertility workup. Such physicians will probably be members of the American Society for Reproductive Medicine. For any advanced diagnosis or treatment of infertility, however—including a laparoscopy, drug therapy, or surgery—we recommend a board-certified reproductive endocrinologist.

3. If you trust your family physician, ask for a referral to an infertility specialist—preferably one who is board-certified. If you need to look for a specialist on your own, the Internet can be a wonderful resource. We suggest the following sites. (Note: Though these Web sites contain helpful information, their inclusion does not necessarily imply endorsement by Focus on the Family of the organizations and physicians listed.)

INCIID (International Council on Infertility Information Dissemination)
www.inciid.org
This organization, pronounced "inside," offers a wealth of medical information, statistics, and resources on infertility. It also provides a state-by-state listing of specialists including reproductive endocrinologists. For those without Web access, the mailing address is P.O. Box 6836, Arlington, VA 22206.

American Board of Medical Specialties (ABMS)

www.certifieddoctor.org

This Web site allows you to verify the board certification, status, and location of physicians certified by one or more of the 24 member boards of the ABMS. At this writing the service is free, but requires signing up and logging in.

RESOLVE

www.resolve.org

Among its many services for infertile couples, RESOLVE maintains a list of clinics on this Web site. A fact sheet, "Selecting an Infertility Physician," is also available here. A physician referral service can be accessed by calling the organization's helpline at (888) 623-0744.

American Society for Reproductive Medicine (ASRM)

www.asrm.org

This site allows users to locate members of ASRM, the Society for Reproductive Endocrinology and Infertility, the Society of Reproductive Surgeons, and clinics belonging to the Society for Assisted Reproductive Technology. The site is careful to note that the listing of physicians and facilities is for information only and does not imply endorsement by ASRM.

THE DOCTOR WILL SEE YOU NOW

After you've carefully chosen a physician, it's time to prepare for your initial interview. And remember: *Both* husband and wife need to attend this session.

Be ready to give a complete medical history. Bring a list of *your* questions, too, and feel free to refer to it. In chapter 10 of this book you'll find questions you may want to ask about the physician's respect for human life and sensitivity to your moral values. In addition, ask whether he or she has had training in infertility treatment beyond his or her residency—if you haven't asked already.

Don't hesitate to inquire about the physician's prices. He or she should have a price list for standard infertility tests and treatments, and should share it willingly. Check to see whether the doctor will accept what your insurance coverage pays for a designated service or operation.

Ask for a description and timetable of a thorough infertility evaluation. What should you look for? Dr. William G. Dodds, board-certified reproductive endocrinologist and Director of Michigan Reproductive and IVF Center, told us that a good, basic infertility evaluation includes the following:

> The initial infertility evaluation begins with an in-depth history of the couple. Important information includes age of the couple, length of the infertility problem, prior pregnancy, including any complications, menstrual cycle regularity, and any pelvic pain problems. In addition, medical illnesses, medications being used, history of pelvic infections, family history of infertility, endometriosis, early menopause or familial genetic problems are also examples of important information that needs to be reviewed. A complete physical exam is also an important part of the infertility evaluation.
>
> Infertility testing starts with a focus on three primary areas: sperm quality, ovulation, and tubal patency (open fallopian tubes). These three areas represent approximately 90% of all infertility causes. Testing should begin with a semen analysis and basal body temperature (BBT) graph. If BBT graphs are unclear with respect to ovulation, a mid-luteal progesterone level may be performed.
>
> To document tubal patency a hysterosalpingography (HSG) is obtained. In this test a dye is injected into the uterus and fallopian tubes so that x-rays can determine the shape of the uterus and the

patency of the tubes. The HSG is done between menstruation cessation and ovulation, generally between days 5 and 10 of the menstrual cycle.

Laboratory testing should include thyroid and prolactin hormonal evaluation in all women with cycle irregularity. A cycle day 2 or 3 follicle stimulation hormone (FSH) should be drawn in all women older than 35 years of age and in those with suspected decreased ovarian competence, indicating possible early ovarian failure. (FSH is a hormone released by the pituitary gland that helps to induce ovulation.)

Chlamydia antibody testing is also recommended. A positive chlamydia trachomatis antibody finding should focus more attention on a possible tubal factor problem. We also recommend a post-coital test (PCT). This test is done at mid-cycle before ovulation and tests if the sperm shows normal mobility in the female's cervical mucus.

A basic infertility evaluation can be accomplished within one to two months. Information from this basic evaluation may lead to other testing such as laparoscopy and ultrasound evaluation of the pelvis, sperm antibody testing, and urology referral for more detailed evaluation of the husband.

After the basic evaluation, the couple should consult with the physician to review all test results and discuss options of care. This, I believe, helps them understand their evaluation better and makes them partners in their care. This can also facilitate obtaining a second opinion about any aspects of their evaluation and treatment.

SHOULD YOU EVER CHANGE DOCTORS?

One should never change physicians quickly or lightly. On the other hand, don't stick with a doctor through thick and thin simply because you've invested a great deal of time, effort, and money in using his or her services.

Consider making a switch if one of the following is true:

1. Your doctor is dragging out the testing you need (two months should be plenty for most infertility testing to be completed).

2. Your doctor discourages or doesn't respond to questions about your care, such as timing and results of tests.

3. Your doctor seems insensitive to the emotional impact of your infertility, and this disturbs you.

4. Your doctor displays a sloppy, disorganized approach, gives evasive answers, or raises "red flags" in your mind about his or her methods. For example, one woman discovered through her own research that a single analysis of a sperm sample is not enough to give an accurate reading of sperm count or motility. Her husband, on the basis of only one analysis, had been diagnosed with a low sperm count and motility level. When she showed her research to her physician and asked whether her husband should be retested, the doctor became evasive and defensive. That "red flag" eventually led the couple to a more competent physician.

5. You've asked God to help you honestly separate your frustration with your infertility from your frustration with your physician—but still feel deep dissatisfaction with your medical treatment.

Perhaps you're thinking, "The authors are certainly critical of the medical profession." We apologize if it looks that way. We know most physicians who specialize in infertility treatment are highly gifted, competently trained, compassionate, and devoted to providing the best treatment available. Occasionally we receive letters of complaint about doctors, but far more often we receive notes like this:

It is with great joy and thanksgiving that we write to you. After struggling with unexplained infertility for several years and undergoing two IUI [intrauterine insemination] attempts, God blessed us with a wonderful pregnancy and a healthy son. Throughout the process our physician was terrific. She not only provided expert medical care; she also cared about us as people. We would recommend her in a heartbeat to those in our area who are struggling with infertility.

DON'T LET TIME FLY WHILE YOU'RE HAVING FUN

When we married, we were 24 (John) and 23 (Sylvia). It was John's last year at seminary; since our next year or two would be filled with many changes, it seemed wise to practice birth control until we became more settled.

Sylvia went on "the pill." She stayed on it for about two years until John became the pastor of a church in New Jersey, and our lives became more routine. We decided to begin our family. Sylvia was 25; John was 26.

We did not know—nor did anyone tell us—that our most fertile years were already behind us.

Dr. William G. Dodds makes the following important observation:

Frequently one will hear that one in ten couples will have infertility. Well, that is true if you look at a large percentage of young couples in their 20s. But if you look at couples in their 30s, the percentage of infertility is significantly higher. For couples between the ages of 30 and 35 the percentage of infertility is one in seven; for those between the ages of 35 and 39 the percentage is one in five. For maturing couples between the ages of 40 and 44 the percentage is one in four.[3]

This suggests that married couples ought to consider having children earlier rather than later. When you delay having children, you place yourself at greater risk for fertility challenges.

IGNORANCE ISN'T BLISS

When we began our infertility journey, we looked for resources to help us on our way. Checking our local library, we found precious little.

Today the picture is far different. The landscape is covered with helpful information to encourage infertile couples—including readable medical data and excellent support from a Christian perspective. The Internet alone provides a plethora of resources, including chat rooms and interactive Web sites.

When it comes to dealing responsibly with infertility, ignorance isn't bliss! Become informed by using resources like those suggested throughout this book. Don't be so brave that you think you won't need counsel from those who've traveled before you. Don't be so trusting that you rely solely on your physician for all the information you need. Knowledge is an important ally on this journey.

Perhaps you're saying to yourself, "I feel sick. My spouse and I have already made these blunders. Now we'll never have a baby!"

We didn't write this chapter to make you feel hopeless. We wrote it so that you, better equipped than before, can continue your journey with greater understanding.

None of us has been on this journey before, so we make our share of mistakes along the way. Don't despair!

A wise, elderly father once gave this counsel to an adult son who had made some errors: "Son, the best time for you to have avoided your mistakes was 20 years ago. The next best time is right now!"

3

Why Does Infertility Hurt So Much?

by Sylvia

∞

When Rachel saw that she was not bearing Jacob any children . . .
she said to Jacob, "Give me children, or I'll die!"

Genesis 30:1

During a low point in our infertility journey, I went to the mall and came home in tears. "There are pregnant women everywhere," I wailed to John. "I even saw one woman with two babies in a stroller, and she was as pregnant as a pumpkin. It's just not fair."

Were there really "pregnant women everywhere"? Of course not. But when you're hurting from infertility, your perceptions are faulty. As someone has said, "When you are infertile, everything and everyone seems intent on making you hurt."

In the moving book *Empty Womb, Aching Heart,* a woman named Megan describes the hurt of infertility in a way that only a person who has been there can appreciate:

I am a reasonable woman. I don't cry at weddings or at the movies (*Titanic* didn't even do it for me). But the diaper aisle at the grocery store? Well, that's a different story. The first time it happened, it took me by surprise.

I strolled down the aisle, pushing my cart with the squeaky left wheel, while my eyes scanned the shelves for the brand of toilet paper that was on sale. It wasn't Northern, or Angel Soft. Charmin! Ten cents cheaper for a four-pack—double rolls! I snatched two packages from the shelf and tossed them into my cart. Then I turned, and my gaze caught sight of a baby with eyes as blue as my husband's and hair the same color as mine. She was staring at me from a package of Huggies. My hands clenched the cart handle. My throat tightened. My vision blurred.

What was happening to me? Tears pooled in my eyes and began to trickle down my cheeks. I grabbed a tissue from my purse and dashed them away, while thoughts, unbidden, unwanted, raced through my mind. Our daughter might have looked like her. That baby could have been mine. When will God bless us with a child? Will God ever bless us? And how can I bear it if he doesn't?[1]

FEELING ALONE

John and I have received enough letters from infertile couples over the years to fill a file cabinet. Of all the feelings woven into these letters, none is more prominent than the isolation many couples experience as they struggle with their inability to be parents. I'll let them express it in their own words:

> . . . In my circle of friends, and the circle outside of that circle, I am the only one I know who is experiencing the difficulty of conceiving.

. . . Although the Lord helps through His Word and prayer, I still feel like I am the only one going through this.

. . . I feel apart from the other women in our church, who are my age. All of them are moms! Even at church, a place where I always felt I "belonged," I really feel "out on my own."

. . . We are in need of help. I have just gone through my third failed IUI attempt with Clomid. I am just devastated. I feel so alone, cursed, crushed, and forgotten by everyone . . . including God.

"JUST RELAX!"

For those facing infertility, pain can come from any direction. Sometimes it takes the form of insensitive comments and advice from those whose lives crisscross our own—including relatives and friends. Everyone from Uncle Harry to sister Mary knows what we ought to do.

Recently John and I—with the help of some infertile friends—made a "Top Ten" list of comments infertile couples hate to hear. Perhaps you could add your own favorites to this list:

10. "Guess who's pregnant—again!"
 9. "It will happen when you're ready."
 8. "So-and-so prayed, and they got pregnant right away."
 7. "You're being too sensitive." (Or, "Maybe you're not meant to have children." Or, "Just accept it and go on." Or, "Stop crying." Or, "We all have problems.")
 6. "Do you want me to give you a few pointers? (Ha, ha!) Are you sure you know how babies are made?"
 5. "I get pregnant so easily! My husband just looks at me and a baby is on the way."

4. "You're lucky you don't have kids." (Or, "Why do you want them, anyway?" Or, "I'll gladly give you a couple of mine." Or, "You don't know how nice you have it—your house never gets dirty.")

3. "You're not getting any younger." (Or, "When are you going to have kids, anyway?" Or, "Are you really so selfish that you don't want any children?")

2. "Adopt! You'll get pregnant for sure."

1. "Just relax! You're trying too hard." (Or, "You're thinking about it too much." Or, "Go on a vacation." Or, "Take a cruise.")

No one intends to hurt those struggling to become pregnant, but hurts happen nonetheless. Once, while I was holding my little niece after a Sunday morning worship service, an elder in our congregation came up to me with a big smile on his face. "You look good with a baby," he said. Turning to John, he whispered loudly, "Maybe now she'll get the idea that it's time for you to have children."

I never held another infant at church or in front of any other group. I know this man didn't mean to hurt me, but he did.

DASHED HOPES

Hurt also happens when hopes are dashed again and again. Each time a period is a few days late, hopes rise—only to fall once more. An anonymous poem expresses so well the hopes and disappointments I so often felt:

> I am in pain.
> Someone just died.
> Who, you say?
> Someone who never was.
> I am infertile.
> My period just came.

I hurt so much.
My own body
Keeps reminding me
That I am incomplete,
I don't function properly.
Why? Why? Why?
Oh, my baby,
Why can't you be?

Even more difficult emotionally are medical procedures that fail to result in pregnancy. Every try at *in vitro* fertilization (IVF), for example, is a time of sky-high hope for many couples; after all, they invest a lot in each attempt. If it fails—and there's at least a 50 percent chance it will—the blow can be crushing.

Recently Karen and her husband scraped together another $10,000 for a third IVF. When they received the disappointing news that it too had failed, I sympathized: "Oh, Karen, I'm sure your emotions have hit the basement."

"Oh, Sylvia," she said with a sigh. "I'm way below the basement."

It is not by accident that many couples describe their infertility as a roller coaster of emotions. Indeed, couples can experience soaring optimism followed by swooping plunges to the depths of despair.

OUT OF THE BEDROOM AND INTO THE DOCTOR'S OFFICE

Couples being treated for infertility soon discover another source of stress, strain, and emotional pain. They find that there is a third person in their marriage.

The unseen but very real presence of the infertility specialist can be felt by practically every one of these couples. Even in their most tender moments, the presence is lying between them and dictating the expression of their love. Like an unwelcome conscience, the presence often whispers in their ears, "Not tonight, lovebirds. Remember, ovulation is scheduled to occur on Friday." On nights when neither party feels very amorous, the presence can almost be heard asking insistently, "Do you want to have a baby or not?"

The dutiful couple is expected to document how often and when the love act has occurred. Husband and wife may wonder, "Did we do it often enough last month? Did we hit the right days? Will our doctor think we don't love each other?"

We don't mean to imply that any of this is the doctor's fault. It's simply that treatment for infertility demands the physician's medical involvement in a couple's sex life.

Knowing it's necessary, however, doesn't make the intrusion any more comfortable. The sex act between a husband and wife represents the culmination of the intimacy God intended for married couples. Ideally, it should remain a private moment. But spouses with fertility issues find that their sex lives have been transported from an intimate, cozy bedroom to the cold, sterile confines of a medical clinic.

THE HIGH COST OF HIGH TECH

Testing and treatment take their toll financially as well as emotionally. Dealing with infertility can be expensive indeed.

Recently, for example, a friend went to the hospital for a laparoscopy. She checked in at 8 A.M. and was home by 2 P.M. The bill was almost $4,000.

Thankfully, her insurance paid a percentage. But the standard operating policy of many insurance companies precludes payment for infertility testing and treatment; it's considered elective, non-essential. Some even consider it to be, in some weird sense, "cosmetic surgery."

Hospital bills, lab tests, and exotic fertilization techniques aren't the only costs infertile couples face, either. One woman told me that she and her husband are spending up to $2,000 a month for fertility drugs.

The expenses might be easier to take if the results were guaranteed. They are not. No one can say whether taking Clomid or other medications will result in a successful pregnancy. The same is true of higher-tech treatments. The world's best IVF clinics, for example, are only averaging a 50 percent success rate at this writing, and some clinics are closer to 25 percent. How long can a couple with limited income pump thousands—or tens of thousands—of dollars into treatment whose success is uncertain?

IS THERE HOPE?

The hurts and hassles of infertility can't be denied. But my purpose in describing them is not to plunge you into despair. I simply know that what Phil Nienhuis, a professional family therapist, says is true: "One cannot begin to recover from pain, until he or she is willing to own the pain and acknowledge that it is real."

Hope and help are on the way—in the next chapter.

4

How Can You Cope While You Hope?

by Sylvia

There are no simple solutions for dealing with the frustrations and pain of infertility. But that doesn't mean that all you can do is sit back and suffer.

In this chapter and the next, you'll discover a variety of strategies for coping—as you continue hoping.

STRATEGY 1: NOURISH RELATIONSHIPS WITH THOSE WHO UNDERSTAND

Dr. Anthony Labrum, an ob/gyn who specializes in infertility, stresses that infertile couples should avoid self-imposed isolation. Husbands and wives need to feel free to talk to someone about their problems, he says, without fearing that what they say may make their listeners uncomfortable.

I wholeheartedly concur! It's vital to find other couples or individuals with whom you can share mutual concerns. Since about one of six couples will experience an infertility problem, there are probably people in your church or circle of acquaintances who face the same kinds of challenges you do.

At the very least, find one person with whom you can feel free to talk about problems in an atmosphere of mutual trust and understanding. To carry the burden of infertility and not be able to share your frustrations with others who understand can add to your sense of desolation.

STRATEGY 2: FIND OR FORM A SUPPORT GROUP

During the height of my struggle with infertility, I met two other Christian women through my contacts with RESOLVE, a national infertility support organization. We talked often. Eventually we formed a support group. It was one of the most helpful steps I took in coming to grips with the difficulties of infertility.

Stepping Stones, the infertility ministry of Bethany Christian Services, maintains a list of local support groups on its Web site. Check www.bethany.org/step for a group that may be meeting in your area.

You may want to check with RESOLVE, too. One of the primary functions of this organization's local chapters is to establish infertility support groups. These groups usually consist of four to eight infertile couples or individuals who are willing to learn from and support each other. Since RESOLVE is a secular organization, you're likely to meet folks there who are from a variety of faith backgrounds. To contact RESOLVE, access their Web site at www.resolve.org or call (888) 623-0744.

If you can't find a good support group in your area, consider starting one. Yes, it's work—but you, and those who join you, will find that the effort yields new friendships that energize and heal.

If you decide to begin a support group, here are some suggestions based on personal experience:

• Start small. Your group can begin with just two people who share a goal. Even if it never grows larger than three or four, the group can still be a wonderful source of support.

• Get help. Stepping Stones offers a packet of information for finding support, including ideas for beginning a support group. E-mail Stepping Stones at step@bethany.org, or call (616) 224-7488. Or contact Hannah's Prayer, P.O. Box 5016, Auburn, CA 95604-6016. This ministry offers a handbook on beginning a support group. You can also reach Hannah's Prayer on the Web at www.hannah.org.

• Choose your meeting place carefully. You might assume your church would be an ideal place to gather. Consider, however, that not everyone may be comfortable there. Like it or not, infertility is often viewed as a very private matter. Even a member of your congregation may think, *I'd like to go to the support group, but I don't want others in our church to see me walking into that room—it would be embarrassing!* Those outside your church may hesitate to go to an unfamiliar place of worship—or any church building. A more neutral choice might be a physician's office, or a community room in a bank or government facility.

• Advertise! Publicize your group through church bulletins, newspapers, radio and TV public service announcements, and fliers in physicians' waiting rooms. Make sure your group is listed with Stepping Stones and Hannah's Prayer. If local news outlets haven't done a story on infertility recently, suggest that they do a report.

• Encourage ownership. To give members a sense of belonging, ask them to help by sending out reminder notices, leading devotionals, organizing a book table, bringing refreshments, starting a prayer chain, or arranging for speakers.

• Bring in the experts. Good candidates for speakers include gynecologists, reproductive endocrinologists, adoption social workers, and panels discussing various aspects of adoption. A pastor could talk about spiritual issues involved in infertility. And speaking of pastors, you might also invite several clergymen from your community to a meeting where they could gain insight into the world of infertility.

• Let people tell their stories. Allow time at each meeting for personal interchange among group members. Healing occurs when couples have the opportunity to share what they've been going through. Whenever we at Stepping Stones sponsor an infertility conference, the only consistent complaint we receive is that many attendees would like more time just to talk with others who understand.

• Use study materials. If including Bible study is appropriate for your group, I recommend *Living with Infertility* by Roger and Robin Sonnenberg (Concordia Publishing Co., 1994). It's available through Christian bookstores or through Stepping Stones (800-613-3188).

STRATEGY 3: GET ONLINE SUPPORT

Through the Internet you can connect with others a world away. Several chat rooms, discussion forums, and e-mail support groups are available, including the following:

Stepping Stones Discussion Forum
http://stepforums.bethany.org

Participants are invited to post questions, share experiences, and offer helpful information and encouragement.

Hannah's Prayer Ministries
www.hannah.org

This Web site allows participants to chat with other infertile couples who face similar circumstances.

Strategy 4: Spend Time with Energizers

Pastor Bill Hybels of Willow Creek Church tells a story that goes something like this.

One night he came home and his wife said, "Oh, Bill, don't forget—tonight we're invited over to the Millers."

His immediate reaction was to groan and say, "Oh, no, not the Millers! He is so boring! Besides, he always quizzes me about the church and how I think things can be improved. When I go over to the Millers, all I do all evening is sneak a look at my watch to see if it's 9:00 so that we can decently say good night and go home. The minutes drag by when I'm with the Millers."

A week later, his wife told him they were going to a different couple's house for dinner.

"Oh, we're going over to Dennis and Judy's? Good! I always enjoy talking to Dennis. When I'm with him, I don't know where the time goes. Before I realize it, it's midnight and we're still going strong, laughing and joking and having a great time. I leave Dennis and Judy's place feeling energized and not depleted."[1]

Infertility is an extremely depleting experience. The last thing we infertile couples need is to spend time with those who'll deplete us even more. Don't be rude, of course, but carefully consider this question before accepting invitations: "Is there a good chance that we'll leave this social event feeling energized and renewed? Or is there a good chance we'll leave feeling depressed, discouraged, and very tired?"

Of course, there are some social engagements we can't avoid no matter how depleting they may be. But try to maximize involvement with people who help you feel comfortable, relaxed, and ready to face life once more. Minimize time spent with those who add to your pain by talking endlessly about their children or offering well-meant but ill-informed advice.

STRATEGY 5: TAKE A DOSE OF "R AND R"

It may be healthy, on rare occasions, to take a short break from medical treatment if it becomes too emotionally draining. This should never be done without consulting your physician. But a month or more of freedom from a treatment routine may significantly improve your outlook on life.

As one person put it, "Suspending treatment for a couple of months was such a treat! It rejuvenated me physically and allowed me to reconnect with my husband emotionally and sexually. It was great to live like a normal married couple for a while. I felt better prepared to continue the difficult work of infertility treatment."

STRATEGY 6: BE HONEST WITH YOURSELF
AND YOUR PHYSICIAN

Under the stress and strain of infertility treatment, some find themselves playing games with the truth. Tired of programmed, regimented sex, they let a month or two go by without making any effort to hit the "right days." When the time comes to report to the doctor, they're less than candid.

Following a month when our statistics weren't exactly stellar, I felt very uneasy thinking about my upcoming doctor's appointment. Should I skip my appointment? Would it be better to leave my chart at home? Should I lie? Would he ask why we didn't have intercourse on the days he recommended?

Instead of practicing such deceptive and self-defeating behavior, tell your physician exactly how you feel and why. Chances are he or she will understand—and may even recommend a temporary reprieve from treatment until you find the energy to do it right.

Strategy 7: Consider Professional Counseling

One of the most poignant letters we ever received came from a woman mourning the death of her marriage:

> My husband and I have tried for nine years to have a child. After two surgeries, an ectopic pregnancy, and three *in vitro* fertilizations, I am still waiting with empty arms. The only difference is that now I wait alone. My disappointment and determination proved to be too much for my husband, so last Christmas he left me. You can imagine the contradictory feelings I have in celebrating the birth of Christ while grieving the death of my marriage.

We mourn for this woman, and for the husband who didn't feel strong enough to cope with her pain. We wonder whether this couple received any professional counseling. If they had, would their marriage have held together?[2]

If you experience severe stress from infertility, don't hesitate to seek professional counseling. You or your physician may find that therapy is necessary to work through severe tension in your marriage or issues of depression and anxiety.

Unfortunately, not all therapists understand the unique pressures that can plague a marriage in which infertility is a primary stressor. Select a counselor carefully. You may wish to check with infertility clinics in your area; some might have counselors on staff, or counselors to whom they refer. Your primary care physician also may be able to refer you to a therapist.

The following organizations may be able to help you find a Christian counselor in your area:

American Association of Christian Counselors (AACC)
www.aacc.net
P.O. Box 739
Forest, VA 24551

Christian Association for Psychological Studies (CAPS)
www.caps.net
P.O. Box 310400
New Braunfels, TX 78131-0400

Focus on the Family
www.family.org
8605 Explorer Drive
Colorado Springs, CO 80920
(719) 531-3400

Focus on the Family also provides professional counseling (a free, one-time service by phone) and referrals to Christian counselors nationwide. The phone line is open weekdays, 9 A.M. to 4:40 P.M. mountain time; ask for the counseling department at extension 2700.

STRATEGY 8: PRACTICE POWERFUL PRAYER

We'll address issues concerning prayer and infertility in a later chapter, but for now I simply want to encourage you with this thought: If frustration, pain, and difficult decisions are gnawing away at your emotional reserves, there's a power available to help. When you consistently take your concerns to the Lord, you plug into the power you need to cope effectively.

Evelyn Christenson, author of *What Happens When Women Pray,* expresses this truth in a story:

One day my husband [a pastor] walked out of the sanctuary of our church and encountered our custodian fairly dripping with perspiration. He was a giant of a Christian, but was gradually losing his ability to think and work because of hardening of the arteries. As my husband saw him struggling with the vacuum cleaner, he looked down, and there lying on the floor was the plug. The dear man had vacuumed the whole auditorium and didn't have the plug in the outlet!

Isn't that what happens to many of us! We work, we pull, we struggle, and we plan until we're utterly exhausted, but we have forgotten to plug into the source of power. And that source of power is prayer. . . .[3]

When you're trudging down the road of infertility, it's easy to forget the power that's only a prayer away. But it holds the greatest potential to help you cope—and hope.

5

Handling the Holidays

by Sylvia

As each Christmas season approaches, society seems to scream in our ears, "Christmas is just around the corner. Come on, be happy! Get into the Christmas spirit. Smile!"

When the cradle is empty, handling the holidays can be a difficult task. There is no magic formula that can heal the hearts of couples who have no child to delight on Christmas morning. But by planning, you can be better prepared. You may even discover some creative, fun ways to celebrate Christmas—and other special days—in your own unique fashion.

THE FIVE WAYS OF CHRISTMAS

If you're dreading the next holiday season, here are some suggestions for your "shopping" list.

1. Remember what it's all about. Focus on the real meaning of the

holiday, not on how difficult it may be for you. The purpose of many holidays, such as Thanksgiving, Christmas, and Easter, is the worship of our great God and Savior. As Dr. James Dobson has written regarding Christmas,

> Each family is allotted a finite number of holiday seasons in a life-time, and each of them is priceless beyond measure. When those days are concluded, perhaps unexpectedly, no power on earth can reunite us for another time of fellowship and worship at the feet of the Christ-child. Don't let the opportunity of this season slip through your fingers as [this season] draws to a close.[1]

Remember that a family can have two members—and that "holidays" are meant to be "holy days."

2. Be selective about the invitations you accept. If you choose not to attend all the family gatherings within a 500-mile radius, don't feel guilty. Sometimes we have to concentrate on our needs and helping our spouses get through the holidays, rather than exposing ourselves to painful reminders of our empty arms. Don't feel you have to say yes to everything.

If you attend a holiday gathering that proves painful for you, consider leaving early. You don't have to "tough it out" to the bitter end.

3. Recognize and accept your feelings of loss and grief over what might have been. These are legitimate emotions.

While it's okay to shed a tear and experience some sadness during the holidays, try not to dwell on those feelings. This may be a good time to commit yourself to the Twenty-Minute Rule (more on this in the next chapter). When you feel sad, discouraged, or angry, allow yourself to deal with it for 20 minutes—but no more. Cry if you must, share your frustration with your spouse, or call a friend—but only for 20 minutes. Don't allow the burden of infertility to ruin your whole holiday season.

4. Plan something special. Take the advice of Naomi Angoff, who suggests the following:

> Spend time doing the things you like best—preparing a spectacular meal, taking long walks, going horseback riding, or curling up by the fire with an intriguing novel. Plan a special trip for just the two of you—a ski weekend, a luxurious resort vacation, a few nights at a cozy country inn. You may have to put up with comments like, "How can you be so selfish?" or "Christmas dinner just won't be the same without you," but those remarks may be easier to tolerate than a holiday table packed with happy children, none of them yours. Begin your own family traditions: a special ceremony or ritual which says the two of you are already a family and you can rejoice in your love for each other, with or without children.[2]

5. Lend a helping hand. Follow the example of Jesus, who said, "For even the Son of Man did not come to be served, but to serve" (Mark 10:45).

Reach out to others in need. Visit an elderly relative. Help dish up a meal at a rescue mission. Spend time at a nursing home. Scripture says, "It is more blessed to give than to receive" (Acts 20:35). Often in giving—especially when we give of ourselves—we receive a blessing. Don't close the door to the positive feelings that come from helping others in Jesus' name.

MOTHER'S DAY: OUCH!

For a woman facing infertility challenges, there's only one holiday more difficult than Christmas. Consider the following scene.

It's Mother's Day. Rachel and her husband, Ted, drive up to their church for the morning worship service. Rachel can't help but notice pretty little girls walking into the building hand-in-hand with their moms. She sees active little boys proudly walking next to their dads. She wonders, *Will that ever be us someday?*

As Rachel and Ted walk into the sanctuary, the display behind the pulpit immediately catches Rachel's eye. Apparently someone on the church decorating committee thought it would be nice to adorn the platform with a selection of baby dolls. Baby dolls in strollers, baby dolls playing, baby dolls sleeping—it's an artistically arranged reminder of Mother's Day and the blessing of having children.

Many in the congregation smile as they view the backdrop. Rachel can't bear to look.

The pastor has chosen to give a message based on Psalm 127. As Rachel hears the beautiful words, she's disheartened.

"Sons are a heritage from the LORD, children a reward from him," the pastor says cheerfully, reading from verse 3. He goes on to state that a child is the greatest blessing God can bestow on a good and happy marriage. "A child is a climax to a godly marriage," he declares. "God's reward."

Rachel is no longer disheartened—she's dismayed. *What about those of us who can't have children?* she wonders with silent sobs. *Is he implying that we don't have a good marriage?*

On the way home from church, Rachel can no longer weep silently. Slowly at first, then in a steady torrent, tears stream from her eyes. She weeps for the baby she has never held; she weeps for the insensitivity of her pastor and her church; she weeps for a husband who not only bears his own pain but tries to be strong for her; she weeps for being so weak that she's allowed herself to be hurt—again.

After a few minutes, Rachel begins to pull herself together. After all, she mustn't have red and swollen eyes when they arrive at Ted's parents' house for Mother's Day dinner. Everyone there will be delighted with the newest baby in the family; no one will want to see Rachel's tears.

"Happy Mother's Day," she sighs quietly, drying her eyes.

A PROACTIVE APPROACH

Mother's Day and Father's Day are the two most difficult days of the year for many couples who have an empty cradle. Is there any plan that can lessen the heartache?

These holidays will always be painful for those struggling with infertility or pregnancy loss. But you don't have to be a passive victim as you face these special days. You can be positively proactive.

Consider Ted and Rachel. Here are some steps they could take:

1. They could recognize that a feeling of ambivalence is normal. Speaking for many of us, one person said, "I want to rejoice with mothers on this special day—I truly do! It's just so difficult when my own arms are empty."

Another said, "In my head I can rejoice with my sisters and brothers in church when they celebrate Mother's Day. It's just that my heart is having trouble keeping pace with my head."

2. They could consider "flight" as a coping mechanism. If attending the Mother's Day service in one's own church proves to be extremely painful for a couple, why not think about visiting another church where there is less focus on the holiday and more focus on worship?

If necessary, a hurting couple might choose to skip church on Mother's Day. I believe God will understand. Is it truly worship to sit through a service where everything seems to worsen your hurt?

3. They could educate others. No one intentionally hurts an infertile couple; it's unlikely that the worship committee thought about how the baby-doll display might affect the childless. But the same thing may happen again next year, unless Ted and Rachel speak up.

Instead of suffering silently, they need to contact the worship committee and patiently describe the impact this display had on them.

4. They could watch for faulty theology. The pastor of Ted and Rachel's church probably didn't realize that he was misapplying Scripture.

Psalm 127 does remind us that children are a blessing from God. But is the opposite true? If a couple with a baby is blessed, does it mean that a couple without a baby is cursed? Absolutely not!

Dr. James Dobson once put it this way: "If a child is evidence of God's blessing, then is the absence of a child evidence of God's disapproval? I think not." Yet many women draw the conclusion that childlessness must be divine punishment. Avoid the self-doubt, guilt, and discouragement that come from believing false theology.

5. They could focus on the positive side of Mother's Day. You may not be a mother, but everyone has a mother. Focus on what your mother has meant to you, even if she hasn't been perfect. Give thanks to God for the blessings you've received from her. If she's alive, show her how much you appreciate her.

"You're Not a Mom!"

Whenever Mother's Day sneaks up on me, I remember my first awareness of how painful this holiday can be.

One Mother's Day I was encouraging the members of my fourth-grade Sunday school class to be thankful for the moms God had given them. One of the 10-year-olds, unaware that she was wielding a dangerous weapon, said offhandedly, "It's not Mother's Day for you—you're not a mom."

It was just a careless comment from a child. I should have shrugged it off. But I was shattered.

Since then, many Mother's Days have come and gone. Not all of them have been equally painful, but none has been easy.

Even now, having become a mom through two adoptions and a surprise pregnancy, I still find it difficult to celebrate Mother's Day. It's not that I'm an ungrateful parent—I love my kids deeply. But every Mother's Day I'm reminded of those who wait and wonder, "Will the day ever come when I'm called 'Mom'?"

Outwardly, I enjoy Mother's Day. But in my heart I cringe, because I know that . . .

• Somewhere a woman hears a child say, "It's not Mother's Day for you—you're not a mom."

• Somewhere a woman leaves a worship service in tears because every mother in church received a rose.

• Somewhere a husband and wife grieve silently because no one knows how much they hurt after yet another negative test or lost pregnancy.

• Somewhere a pastor eloquently prays for mothers, children, and families, but never mentions those who are unable to conceive or give birth.

Yet I do more than cringe on this day. I also pray. I pray that you, if you long to be a mother or father, will in time be blessed by the music of children in your ears. Even more than that,

I pray that out of his glorious riches [God] may strengthen you with power through his Spirit in your inner being, so that Christ may dwell in your hearts through faith. And I pray that you, being rooted and established in love, may have power, together with all the saints, to grasp how wide and long and high and deep is the love of Christ, and to know this love that surpasses knowledge— that you may be filled to the measure of all the fullness of God.

Ephesians 3:16-19

6

How to Keep Your Marriage Strong

by John and Sylvia

It's a beautiful summer evening as George and Helen drive home from the lake. They and the rest of the clan gathered today for a birthday party at the cottage owned by George's parents. Little Megan, beautiful daughter of George's younger sister, just turned one.

To celebrate their first grandchild's birthday, George's parents pulled out all the stops. There were balloons, teddy bears, a huge cake, and enough food to feed a small nation.

It was obvious to Helen that George really enjoyed the party. Laughing and joking with his brothers and sisters, he didn't seem to mind the barb thrown out by his brother: "Well, George, maybe you should spend less time on the golf course and more time working on a family." George just chuckled, but Helen smarted deeply.

Now, as they drive home in silence, Helen thinks about how difficult the party was for her. How could George have enjoyed himself so much? Didn't he realize how hurt she was? Why does she feel so alone?

Without intending to, Helen begins to sob. George, who's been fiddling with the radio to see if he can catch the end of the Chicago Cubs game, is dumbfounded. He simply doesn't know what to make of his wife's tears.

He stops the car, switches his brain into "computer mode," and runs a quick scan of possible reasons for Helen's meltdown. Did he forget that today was an anniversary? Did he do something to upset her?

Finally George asks in desperation, "Why are you so upset? Just tell me—I don't have a clue!"

Closer Together or Further Apart?

Infertility delivers a massive dose of stress in many marriages. George and Helen are among the couples who find that infertility is pulling them apart rather than drawing them closer together.

On the other hand, we're convinced that in some marriages the experiences of infertility and miscarriage draw a couple closer together. As two letter writers put it:

> Following our failed IVF attempt, my husband held me in his arms, telling me not to be afraid. I realized how blessed I was to have a Christian husband and true soul mate. I was determined to enjoy and appreciate our lives together, celebrating today and not worrying too much about tomorrow. God knew when the right time would be for us.

> At this time of year, when we are to remember Christ's birth, we are reminded that this would have been our child's first Christmas. I know our child is with Christ, and we will get to see him one day. My husband, Jim, and I have gone through a lot over the past two

years. Jim's strength has pointed me to Christ when I got lost in my grief. For all of these pains we have gone through, we were able to grow so much together.

Research tends to confirm this paradox. Frank van Balen, one of the few researchers to study the impact of infertility on marriage, suggests that the stress childlessness puts on a relationship can lead to either strengthening or separation.[1]

If infertility has strengthened your marriage and moved you to a higher level of marital understanding and loving relationship with your spouse, you can skip the rest of this chapter. You don't need it. Praise God!

But if the trials and tribulations of infertility are threatening to put distance between yourself and the one you love, read on. This chapter is for you!

As the adage says, "Forewarned is forearmed." That's why we're about to alert you to several dangers that may stalk your marriage—and a survival kit that can protect you against them.

THE BLAME GAME

When a marriage experiences infertility, there's a tendency, subtly or not, to focus on "who's to blame." As a result, one partner may feel superior and the other inferior. One may feel disappointment over the other's "inadequacies," while the other feels guilt for the same. One partner may be relieved that he or she is not "the problem," while the other becomes depressed because she or he *is*.

As John recalls,

For us this was a significant problem. I well remember the first time Sylvia suggested that I go to my doctor for a semen analysis.

I nearly choked on my applesauce. "You want *me* to be checked?" I exploded. "But I sent *you* to the doctor!" It was, frankly, a blow to my masculinity—and I admitted it. "You can handle it better if there is something wrong with you," I said. "It's easier for a woman."

She wasn't so sure about that. By the end of the day, I agreed to the test. I took my sample to the lab the next morning.

The following week Sylvia went to the doctor to get the report on a biopsy she'd undergone, and to see if the results were back from my semen analysis. They were. Much to her surprise, she learned that the problem might not be all hers. She'd passed her test with flying colors, but the doctor recommended I consult a urologist and have my sperm analysis repeated.

Sylvia confided later that it was a load off her shoulders. *Ha, ha,* she chuckled to herself. *It might not be me after all, but you, John.*

Needless to say, I was crushed. I honestly felt it was a greater blow to me because I was a male.

"Nonsense!" Sylvia said. She tried to explain how she'd felt when she'd been sure the problem was all hers. If she couldn't give me children, she felt she was not a complete woman and would be letting me down. At times she even wondered if I was sorry I'd married her.

Infertility is a *couple's* problem. It's one of the few known medical conditions that involve two people! The trouble isn't an infertile wife or an infertile husband, but an infertile couple. Until you understand that fact, you may experience a great deal of solitary and unnecessary pain.

God said that "a man will leave his father and mother and be united to his wife, and they will become one flesh" (Genesis 2:24). Becoming "one flesh" refers to much more than the sex act; it means that a husband and wife work at being "one" in sharing their hopes, dreams, and joys— as well as the burdens, sad times, and challenges.

COMMUNICATION COLLAPSE

Communication between husband and wife is crucial if the stresses that accompany infertility are to be dealt with effectively. Consider the following example.

Bill and Jan were married shortly after high school. On their farm they worked side by side, day in and day out, growing closer. They helped each other through several family crises. They talked about most everything, including their infertility.

But when Jan brought up the subject of adoption, Bill shut down the discussion. "I don't want someone else's baby!" he said. "Let's just forget it."

Whether Bill's fierce outburst was the result of a bad day at work or just the overall frustration of infertility, we don't know. But we do know that, from that time on, Jan and Bill rarely spoke of their disappointment in being unable to have children.

A few years later Jan began suffering from clinical depression. At first no one understood why. Finally a wise counselor helped Bill and Jan realize that the two of them were hurting because they had no child—but each had been hurting alone.

When one marriage partner feels that he or she doesn't have the other's permission to talk about grief and loss, the result is frustration, anger, and despair. We regularly receive cries for help like the following: "Do you have anyone to talk to? I have nowhere to turn. My church is insensitive and rude. My husband is shattered, but silent."

Is He an H.I.M.?

If you're the female half of a marriage that suffers from infertility and a lack of communication, you may be married to an H.I.M.

What is an H.I.M.? Chris Fabry coined this term in *The H.I.M. Book: A Woman's Manual for Understanding Her Highly Identifiable Male.* In this book Fabry admits to being an H.I.M.—a male who doesn't communicate well, shuns feelings, and makes work his mistress. An H.I.M. can talk for hours about the 1972 World Series, but clams up whenever you want to talk about something important.

In tongue-in-cheek fashion, Fabry provides "The Ultimate H.I.M. Diagnostic Quiz." It's intended for wives who want to know whether or not they're married to an H.I.M. Here it is:

> *Please answer the following questions as true or false.*
> 1. I know more about sea anemones than I do about my husband's feelings.
> 2. My husband's priorities seem to be work, sports, his car, the yard, church . . . and then me.
> 3. My husband would rather floss with razor wire and gargle with shards of glass than discuss our marriage.
> 4. My husband would rather jam his head on the end of a sharpened pencil than go to counseling.
> 5. Sometimes I feel alone in this marriage.
> 6. Okay, I feel alone most of the time in this marriage.
> 7. I can't tell you how alone I feel in this marriage.
> 8. I really wish my husband would significantly change in a few areas.
> 9. My husband is a great person and I love him, but I'm frustrated because we don't seem to be on the same team.

10. I am willing to do just about anything to change our relationship for the better.

If you answered five or more as "true," you are married to an H.I.M.[2]

THERE IS A DIFFERENCE

No question about it—most men and women handle communication differently. But in the case of infertile couples, is it only a matter of style—or substance?

In other words, do husbands and wives simply have different ways of expressing their feelings about infertility—or do they have different reactions to infertility itself? Do wives, for example, tend to feel a greater sense of pain and loss over their inability to be mothers than husbands do over their failure to be fathers?

This is a controversial question. Each time we speak to infertility groups on this issue, it raises a flood of disagreements. Still, the majority response is usually something like, "Of course most husbands hurt as much as their wives do, but they just show it differently."

We're convinced, however, that it's not quite so simple. In talking to countless infertile couples, we've found significant differences in the ways husbands and wives view infertility and pregnancy loss.

In our own case, not recognizing those differences caused serious misunderstanding and anger. Sylvia describes how she was feeling:

In the beginning I assumed that John felt the same as I did about the fact that we could not have a baby. I was sure that he must be hurting inside as much as I was, that it bothered him when our friends had a new baby, that he deeply sympathized with me in my weary pregnancy testing and visits to the doctor, and that he understood when I burst into tears for no apparent reason.

In time, however, it became obvious that my assumptions were wrong. John wanted children badly and was very disappointed I did not become pregnant. But I realized that he was not hurting at the depth or with the same intensity that I was. With that realization came anger. Why didn't he show more understanding for what I was going through? Why didn't he put his arms around me the first time I started crying instead of standing there with open mouth, wondering what on earth was wrong with me? Why did he show only lukewarm interest whenever I brought up the subject of our infertility for discussion?

The net result was increased isolation. I not only felt isolated from the people of the fertile world around me, but also increasing detachment from my own husband.

Those feelings of frustration, guilt, anger, and isolation are not unusual. When couples struggle with infertility, it's usually the woman who feels the greater emotional involvement and who tends to suffer more. It's typically the woman who seeks treatment first, and who initiates conversations about "our problem." It's the woman who sees the pregnant lady on every street corner. It's the woman who tends to read the books and magazine articles on infertility—and who, for the most part, writes them.

There are several possible reasons for this. For many women motherhood may remain the number one vocational goal, regardless of a career or job; many women see motherhood as an essential part of their identity. A man, on the other hand, may find identity in being a father—but is more apt to find it elsewhere as well, usually in a career or avid pursuit of a hobby.

Women also tend to be reminded of their childless state far more frequently than men are. Women's magazines, for instance, typically deal with homes and families—while men's magazines deal more often with golf, electronics, fishing, and football. What do women usually end up talking about at church events? You guessed it. What do men talk about? You guessed that, too.

Wives, not husbands, are invited to baby showers. Wives, much more than husbands, are asked: "Well, when are you planning to start your family?" Wives are typically the ones who hear the "exciting news" about friends who just had another baby.

Academic studies also suggest that wives tend to see infertility as a greater heartache than husbands do. In one study, infertile participants were asked whether infertility was the most difficult thing they had to face. Over 57 percent of the women said yes; only 12 percent of the men felt that way. Nearly half the women reported feeling angry over their infertility; only 10 percent of the men said they felt any anger.[3]

In another study, 50 percent of female respondents said their infertility was the greatest burden they had to bear. Just 10 percent of the men said the same thing.[4]

We don't mean to suggest that husbands can't be devastated by infertility. Countless husbands are. One physician, for example, sent us a letter in which he shared the profound impact infertility had made on his life:

> For me it was a grief and loss reaction as severe as any other. It had a very real psychological effect on my whole life. . . . I will always be a member of the group of infertility couples, a group for whom one of life's greatest joys and deepest emotions is but an empty void, a far-off hope.

Another man wrote, "I'll never have a son that I can take to a Promise Keepers event." At the last PK gathering his "heart ached" as he saw "tons of men with their sons."

Still another man expressed his great sorrow that he, as an only son, would not be able to pass on his family name. He felt he was failing his parents.

Some infertile husbands suffer ridicule from friends or coworkers. One man, a high school teacher on a weekend retreat with his colleagues, disclosed the purpose of the medicine he was taking. He thought his fellow teachers would react maturely, but for the rest of the weekend he was the butt of jokes. One colleague laughingly accused him of "shooting blanks," and others made remarks that were less printable. He wrote, "I had no choice but to grin and bear it, but it brought pain."

We don't wish to minimize that. Nevertheless, many wives feel infertility's pain and loss more intensely than their husbands do. Speaking from his many years of treating infertility patients, Dr. Joe S. McIlhaney states:

> The intense pain many infertile women feel about their inability to conceive has led me to conclude that for them having children is as basic a function as eating, breathing, and sleeping. Bearing a child seems to fulfill an essential need of a woman's body and relieves an inner craving. . . . It has helped me as a man, and as a physician, to be aware of the vicious torment infertility inflicts on a woman. . . .[5]

When husbands and wives refuse to recognize that there may be significant differences in the way they view infertility, they're setting themselves up for marital strife. Wives shouldn't assume that their husbands understand the depth of their pain; husbands need to remember that their wives may view motherhood as essential to their fulfillment.

A MARRIAGE SURVIVAL KIT

Many couples who experience infertility discover that their marriage is on a survival mission—and it's not just a training exercise! How can you and your spouse preserve your relationship—and even improve it—during this difficult time?

We recommend a marriage survival kit. Make sure it contains the following items:

1. A Band-Aid

Why? Because it will remind you of an important characteristic of husbands: They like to make things feel better.

Husbands hate to see anything broken—especially their wives, who are hurt by the dashed hopes and crushed dreams that mark infertility. As one husband put it, "The most difficult part is knowing that Linda (my wife) is in so much pain."

In our case, John hated it when Sylvia grieved over our infertility. He hated it so much that he was "Johnny-on-the spot" with "Band-Aid" words and a quick kiss to make it better.

"It will happen," he reassured. "Don't worry, we're still young. We can always try again next month. Why don't you and I go out for dinner this evening so you can get your mind off infertility? Talking about it all the time only makes you depressed. You need to start looking on the bright side of things. After all, you've got me, and we're happy together! Be thankful for what you've got."

Behold: Mr. Fix-it to the rescue! Like John, most husbands think it's their God-given duty to make their wives feel better.

Unfortunately, these husbands tend to downplay the pain. Their motives may be great, but their strategy isn't. Women suffering from infertility don't need someone to *minimize* the pain; they need someone who *understands* it.

Husbands need to learn that they don't have to fix the pain. They can't! More helpful than "fixing" is simply going to your wife, putting your arms around her, and saying, "You're really hurting today, aren't you? I can't make it better, but I want you to know that I love you—and when you hurt, I hurt, too."

2. A Stopwatch

Wives like to talk more than their husbands do. Marriage and family therapist Philip Nienhuis says,

> Studies have indicated that in a typical day a woman will use significantly more words than her husband will use. He will be very matter of fact in stating the experiences of the day, or relating interactions with people he has met. She, on the other hand, will tend to go into much greater detail in reporting experiences or describing relationships. . . .
>
> Many women find it therapeutic to talk—it is a way of relieving stress. Men, on the other hand, often find that talking about an issue produces stress.[6]

Picture this: A husband comes home, exhausted after a challenging day. The only thing he wants to do is hibernate in front of the Monday night football game. The last thing he wants is to talk about infertility—again!

Meanwhile, his wife had a difficult day too. A woman at the office has announced an unexpected, unwanted pregnancy. Devastated by the unfairness of it all, the wife comes home and wants to talk with her husband about how this makes her feel.

What's going to happen when these two come together for the evening? Tension, not tenderness.

Here's where the stopwatch comes in. It can remind a couple of what has often been called the "Twenty-Minute Rule."

As far as we can determine, Merle Bombardieri first came up with the idea in the *National RESOLVE Newsletter*. It's a simple technique designed to let couples talk about infertility without allowing it to dominate the relationship. Having discussed their infertility often and in depth in the past, the couple agrees that if one of them brings up the topic, they'll discuss it for 20 minutes and no longer. After 20 minutes they'll move to another subject.

This is a good rule! When it's practiced, several things happen. The wife knows she has to focus her comments clearly or she'll miss her chance. The husband, instead of listening with one ear while the other is trying to catch the football score, concentrates on what his wife is saying because he knows it's not going to be an all-night conversation. Best of all, they have the rest of the evening to talk about and do other things.

3. Bubble Bath and Candles

For many couples undergoing infertility treatment, romance is an early casualty. Though some report that the experience draws them closer, many find it takes a toll on intimacy and spontaneity.

How can you keep your romance alive? Try little things—a love note in lipstick on the bathroom mirror, a love poem tucked into a briefcase, a night at a cozy bed-and-breakfast, a long evening walk together. Sometimes all it takes is a bit of creativity. We like the way Colleen Botsios describes a romantic evening with her husband:

> Two years ago on Valentine's Day, I was feeling about as low as I had ever been. All the basic infertility workup had been completed and nothing stood out as an obvious impediment to pregnancy. . . . But then, as always, I regrouped. It was Valentine's Day. Time to be festive and romantic.
>
> My husband arrived home for work about 6 P.M. And I met him in a sexy nightgown, explaining that I had a romantic evening planned. I showed him to the bathroom, which was dark except for the votive candles scattered around. The whirlpool was gurgling away in the corner, complete with coconut bubble bath and really hot water. . . .
>
> Somewhere in the special aura of the evening, infertility,

though still close, was somehow far away from us and not so over-whelming. There was temporarily some room to cuddle and smile and laugh heartily.[7]

4. A Cell Phone

Sometimes even the closest of couples run out of patience, hope, or energy. When the challenges of infertility tax your resources to the limit, help can be just a phone call away. Don't hesitate to consult a counselor or pastor, even if it's just for a few sessions to get your relationship back on track.

For guidance on finding a counselor, see the organizations listed at the end of chapter 4.

PEACHES AND PLUMS

Thankfully, many of us have spouses who understand and care. In such marriages there's a wonderful sense of making the journey of infertility together. Partners hurt together, pray together, and support one another as they face the challenges of infertility or miscarriage.

In these marriages, husbands accompany their wives to doctors' appointments and are present for every procedure. They bring their wives a bouquet or arrange for a dinner out on those dark days when gloom is running high and hope is running low. Husbands like that are "peaches."

And in these marriages, wives understand their responsibility to sup-port their husbands—especially when the husband appears to have the main medical problem. These wives know that being told by a physician, "You're not in the major leagues in terms of sperm production or motil-ity," or, "I'm afraid you're sterile," is a blow to any man.

These wives know the last thing their husbands need are comments like, "I told you a long time ago you should be checked," or, "You knew you should have been wearing boxer shorts, but you're too stubborn."

A husband needs a wife who, using her God-given charm and grace, helps him to know that he's still sexy, strong, and valued. Such a wife is a "plum"!

Whether your spouse has told you or not, he or she is counting on you. Your marriage can thrive—if you renew your commitment to be the wife or husband your partner needs.

7

What Do You Say to Aunt Sally?

by John and Sylvia

I was a sixth grade teacher in a small town school. Because of the stresses of teaching while trying to get pregnant, I made the decision to leave teaching. In a conversation with my principal, I told her that I was leaving teaching to start a family. A few weeks later, with many children, teachers, and parents in the building, my principal announced over the intercom that I was trying to get pregnant. As a result, even months later, I would run into parents of students I didn't even have in my room . . . they would look at me and say, "Oh, you are still not pregnant!" The humiliation of an entire town knowing my personal life is more humiliating than I can even believe.

—From a letter received by Sylvia

As this note illustrates, infertility puts a strain not only on your emotions and your marriage, but on your relationships with others as well.

How can you deal with well-meaning but sometimes insensitive friends, family, and fellow Christians? What should you tell them about your infertility, and how? And what should you do if they hurt you?

What Do You Say to a Friendly Lady?

Perhaps the first question to answer is this: How should you deal with curious strangers? For example, what do you say to the cheerful young woman who sits across from you at the company picnic, or the friendly grandma sitting next to you on the airplane?

You know the scenario. You begin a conversation. She asks where you live and what you do, and you ask her in return. Eventually she raises the question, "How many children do you have?"

For most people this question is no more threatening than being asked if they would like a piece of gum. But those struggling with infertility may find it tough to handle. On the one hand, to say simply that you don't have any children may leave the impression that you are one of *those* people—self-centered, career-oriented, someone who simply can't be bothered with the mundane responsibility of raising children. Even if the other person is not thinking that (and most often he or she is not), you might assume the worst. On the other hand, it's unnecessary to explain your childless state to someone you've never met before and probably will never meet again.

If you're trying to have a child but haven't yet been successful, say something like, "None yet, but we're still hoping." If you're beyond the point of childbearing, you could say something like, "No, unfortunately, we were never blessed with any."

Responses like these do two things: They answer the question and avoid wrong assumptions.

WHAT DO YOU SAY TO AUNT SALLY?

By far the greater problem is learning how to handle the attitudes and remarks of people close to us—good friends and members of the family.

Most infertile couples' friends and family members would never intentionally hurt them. Yet seemingly innocent things—like trying to cheer the childless couple by telling them "how lucky they are" or calling them in ecstasy every time someone has a newborn—can add salt to the wound. Then there's the problem of being invited to gatherings where children are the primary topic of conversation.

Here are several approaches you can try to help lessen the hurt that friends and family members may bring into your life.

1. *Don't remain silent.* Not wanting to be open with strangers and casual acquaintances about your longing to have a baby is one thing. But keeping friends and family members completely in the dark is quite another.

Many infertile couples do the latter. They're embarrassed to let others know they have a problem. Some feel guilty about it, as if they're responsible for the fact that their bodies aren't working perfectly. For whatever reason, they see infertility as something that must never be discussed.

We'd like a nickel for every time a husband and wife have told us they've been struggling with infertility—and that no one around them knows! None of their friends, siblings—or, in some cases, even parents—know.

The Bible says, "Carry each other's burdens, and in this way you will fulfill the law of Christ" (Galatians 6:2). But how can others do this if they don't know about the burden you carry?

Many couples have endured unnecessary hurt simply because they haven't told close friends and family members that they're facing an infertility problem. Once you share with parents, siblings, and friends that you're trying to have a baby and are getting medical help, it's amazing what can happen. Often the silly questions disappear, the "funny" jokes cease, and the supposedly friendly jibes are never again launched.

We've always tried to be open about our infertility with friends and family. In return we've seldom experienced the kind of hurt that's often felt by those who keep their infertility a secret sorrow.

A friend shared this experience:

It was at the annual family reunion that my sister-in-law, Jane, shared the unexpected news that she was pregnant. It was difficult for me to hear, but after ten years of experiencing infertility in my life, I had learned to live with such "joyful" news. Shortly after the announcement I worked up the courage to walk over to Jane, and I asked her if she and Mike (her husband) had chosen names already.

"No," she answered, "it's still a bit early, and we're in a state of shock."

"Well," I suggested lightly, "you can feel free to use the names we have picked out; it looks as if we won't need them."

And then for the first time I shared my infertility experience with Jane. She was shocked. Mike's mom had repeatedly assured her that I was into dogs, not kids.

On the other hand, we're not suggesting that couples broadcast their infertility from the rooftops. Selectivity is advised. Couples considering *in vitro* fertilization, for example, may not wish to divulge that fact if they run the risk of a judgmental and uninformed response. Some may also choose to withhold information from friends and relatives who are likely to gossip or become overly inquisitive.

2. *Correct patiently and kindly.* Here's an excerpt from a mother's note to her son and his wife:

Did you hear about Dan and Tracey? I talked to them yesterday
after church to see how their little girl was doing. You knew, didn't
you, that they had adopted a beautiful little girl from Russia? Anyway, Tracey was so excited. I thought you might like to know.
Maybe if you two just adopt, you'll get pregnant?

Sooner or later you, too, will receive useless and irritating advice. A
dear aunt might try to "cheer you up" by telling you about her sister's
niece who was infertile for eight years and now has four kids. A good
friend may suggest that you're "too uptight." Your father may declare,
"You're both still young and healthy; I'm sure it's just a matter of time."

Getting such advice can be exasperating. But we don't believe exaspera-
tion—or its first cousin, anger—is a very helpful or Christlike way to deal
with this kind of situation. Those loved ones mean well. They're honestly
trying to help. Their motive usually is love; their fault is ignorance.

A better approach is to help remove their ignorance by kindly and
tactfully informing them of the facts. The son who received the "adopt
and you'll get pregnant" news flash from his mother could send her a
note along the following lines:

Thanks for the suggestion, Mom, but we have a profound respect
for the adoption process. We believe that to adopt a child in the
hope of getting pregnant is neither fair to the adopted child nor
honoring to God. It implies that adopted children are "second
best" rather than viewing adopted children as wonderful and ful-
filling blessings in their own right. Besides, statistics show that
couples who adopt are not more likely to give birth than couples
who don't adopt.[1]

3. *Remember that those close to you may hurt too.* This is an important
caution, especially in dealing with your parents. You may grieve the fact

that you have no child; they may mourn because they have no grand-child. Infertility may threaten their hopes as well as yours.

Some parents also may carry guilt over their children's infertility. Take the case of people we'll call Jennie and Joe:

Joe's parents know all about our infertility problems. We had kept them informed on what was wrong and which doctor we were see-ing. We must have told them a dozen times that I was perfectly healthy (as far as the doctor could determine) but that Joe had an extremely low sperm count and poor motility. We had also told them that the doctor speculated that the problems might have resulted from a childhood bicycle accident in which Joe's scrotum had been injured and an infection had set in.

Even though we had told Joe's parents over and over again what the main problem seemed to be, every time we talked to them about our infertility, Joe's mother would ask, "Didn't they find anything wrong with Jennie?" After about the fourth time in a year that this question popped up, Joe and I became very irri-tated. Thankfully, we tried not to let it show.

One night after talking about the attitude of Joe's mother, both of us came to the same conclusion. Joe's mother felt guilty. She blamed herself for Joe's near sterility. When it became apparent that we were probably not going to have a baby, Joe's mother probably said to herself a hundred times: "If only I had been more careful about where Joe rode his bike," or "If only we had gotten better medical treatment when Joe injured him-self." After thinking this all through, Joe and I concluded that his parents almost hoped there was something wrong with me because then they would not feel solely responsible for our infertility.

WHAT DO YOU SAY TO YOUR FELLOW BELIEVERS?

The church should be a sanctuary and place of healing. Unfortunately, it can become an unwitting culprit in causing hurt to the infertile couple.

Consider the following announcements that came from an actual church bulletin:

Emphasis on the Christian Family: May 2 to June 20

May 2	Parent's Day
May 9	Mother's Day
May 15, 16	Marriage Enrichment Weekend
May 23	Children's Day
May 30	Singles Day
June 6	Senior Adults Day
June 13	Youth Day
June 20	Father's Day[2]

What's missing from that list? If you face infertility, you know!

Make your church a place where childless couples can say, "This is where I can belong and grow strong." Here are some suggestions:

1. *Keep your expectations realistic.* Not everyone in your church will recognize the depth of pain caused by infertility. To expect that all will "get it" only sets you up for continual disappointment.

Try to find one or two other people in your congregation who understand. Encourage them to pray for you, as you promise to pray for them (after all, everyone faces some kind of challenge).

2. *Make your pastor an ally.* Most pastors work hard to provide Christ-centered support for people in crisis. But even the most sensitive pastor may not be able to give much support to infertile couples without two things you can supply: encouragement and information.

Unless pastors have personal experience with infertility, they may not think much about the infertile couples in your church—until someone encourages them to do so. Perhaps you are that someone! Remind your pastor that when childless couples hear their needs brought before God in prayer, they'll never forget it. Conversely, if the needs of the childless are never mentioned, they'll never forget that, either! As one church member puts it,

> Thankfully, our church is learning to reach out to those hurting while still honoring mothers. We are so grateful that in recent years our pastor has always prayed for those waiting on the Lord to make them someone's mommy. This acknowledgement means more to us than anything anyone has ever said.

Along with encouragement, provide your pastor with information. Give him a copy of this book and ask him to read sections you've marked as especially important. If you subscribe to *Stepping Stones*, occasionally copy relevant articles from this free newsletter. To subscribe, e-mail step@bethany.org or call 1-800-613-3188 and ask to be put on the mailing list.

One more idea: If Mother's Day services are painful for you, try talking to—or writing to—your pastor before that Sunday arrives. Many pastors are simply not aware of how Mother's Day and Father's Day affect those without children.

Here's a letter that an infertile friend wrote to her pastor. You might want to adapt it and send it to yours.

> Dear Pastor,
> It's almost Mother's Day again. They seem to come so quickly. I'm sure you are planning a very special service for all the mothers. I know that it is such a special day for them, and I do not want to

spoil anyone's joy. It is important for all us to rejoice with each other, and even those of us who are not mothers can give thanks for those who are mothers.

All I ask is that you remember that this day can be extremely difficult for a number of members of our congregation. For women like me who struggle with infertility, Mother's Day can be the most painful day of the year. I've thought about staying home, but I know I need to be in God's house.

The most challenging part of the service is when all the mothers stand and the congregation smiles and applauds them. It feels awful to be the only one still sitting. I want to be able to stand with them. I want more than anything in this world to be a mother. It's something I have always wanted. I have carried children, but they were taken before they were ever born. I do have children in heaven, but I am not a mother in the eyes of those here on earth.

So, on Mother's Day I often go home and cry, not quite able to understand why I am unable to become what so many in the church consider to be "God's highest calling" . . . a mother.

It is not only the un-mothers who feel lonely on this day. It must also be a painful day for single women who have never married, for mothers who have lost children, and for moms who have sons or daughters wandering from the Lord.

As Mother's Day approaches, I pray that you will remember that it is not only a day of rejoicing for some, but also a day of painful reminders for others. I know that God will help you to be a blessing to our congregation as you minister to us on this Mother's Day.

And please remember: If your pastor is sensitive to and supportive of those facing infertility or pregnancy loss, express your appreciation!

3. *Learn to say no without feeling guilty.* Whether they need nursery helpers, Sunday school teachers, or youth sponsors, churches often tend to ask infertile couples to help. After all, you have the time, right? Besides, it will give you an opportunity to be with children!

If helping in your church nursery is too painful, don't feel guilty about politely declining. Consider volunteering for another area of service in the church instead. If attending a women's Bible study is difficult because the topic always seems to revolve around parenting, find a study where the focus is broader. Remember that even Jesus sometimes said no to the demands of others in order to take care of Himself physically and spiritually (see Luke 5:15-16).

THEY'RE ONLY HUMAN

The church is made up of people, and people can sometimes disappoint us. That's true of family, friends, and strangers, too.

By keeping your expectations reasonable, sharing appropriate information, and avoiding situations that are bound to cause undue pain, you can deal with the slings and arrows others unwittingly send your way.

People may let us down, but there is One who never will. "God is our refuge and strength, an ever-present help in trouble. Therefore we will not fear . . . " (Psalm 46:1-2).

8

Faith and Infertility: The Nagging Question

by John

For many couples, one question gets at the heart of their spiritual struggle with infertility:

Dear Jesus,

Why can't we have a baby? You know how desperately we want a child. You understand how difficult it is when friends around us have started their families, and they ask us why we don't begin ours. You have seen our tears. You have heard our prayers. Why then have You allowed us to suffer this way? Why haven't You granted us the laughter of little children? Why? Why? Why?

In the correspondence we receive, the "Why?" question is raised more than any other:

Right now I have this huge, gaping hole in my heart. I beg and plead with God for a baby, but there is no response. I don't understand why He is leaving us without children.

Why does God have favorites? Why does He allow movie starlets, promiscuous teenagers, and even prostitutes to have children, while many godly people are barred from having children they would raise for Him?

The "Why?" question is certainly not new, nor is it asked only by the infertile. It's asked by parents who lose their four-year-old daughter to leukemia while the child's 90-year-old grandfather lives on in good health. It's asked by the 23-year-old seminary graduate who's diagnosed with a brain tumor a week before leaving for missionary duty. It's raised by the 30-year-old schoolteacher who hasn't found a life partner though she so desperately wants one.

Knowing that the question isn't unique to the infertile, however, doesn't make it any less real or intense. "Why?" cries out for an answer. Here are some possibilities.

POSSIBILITY 1: A FALLEN WORLD

Bobbie Lynn Smith wants an answer from God. Five years ago she and her husband began infertility testing and treatment. After spending their life savings of $20,000 on medication and two IVF treatments, she and her husband remain childless.

To add insult to injury, her husband was diagnosed with cancer 18 months ago. He is now cancer-free, but the treatment has left him sterile.

She wants to know what God is saying to her and her husband. She wonders, "Is He telling us it isn't His will for us to have children? Does He want us to adopt? Is He preparing us for some miracle? I don't know how to tell."

Like Bobbie Lynn, many of us assume that in each instance of suffering God is trying to tell us something. But is He?

I'm not sure that each time our path takes us through disappointment or trouble God is trying to teach us some specific lesson. I've come to appreciate the perspective Philip Yancey describes in his book *Where Is God When It Hurts?* Yancey writes that he attended a funeral service for a teenager killed in an accident. At the service someone said, "The Lord took her home. He must have had some purpose."

Yancey, however, suggests, "Maybe *God isn't trying to tell us anything specific* each time we hurt." Instead, Yancey believes suffering may be a general message to all who are willing to hear that we live in a fallen world which needs help.[1]

I believe this is the very lesson Jesus wants us to learn from an incident of unexplained suffering described in Luke 13. In that passage Jesus comments on a tower in the village of Siloam that fell and killed 18 people. Jesus asks, "Do you think they were more guilty than all the others living in Jerusalem? I tell you, no! But unless you repent, you too will all perish" (vv. 4-5).

In other words, this world has been so scarred by sin that earthquakes, automobile crashes, accidental drownings, incurable cancer, miscarriages, and infertility are part of the current condition. These things are powerful reminders to anyone who will listen that all of us need a Savior and Redeemer, a Redeemer who will one day make all things well (see Romans 8:18).

At the same time, I believe that for some of us in the fellowship of the infertile, there may be specific lessons God wants us to learn. The remaining four possibilities could apply.

POSSIBILITY 2: TO SHOW THE RESULTS OF DISOBEDIENCE

I want to be extremely careful in discussing this possibility. I know that many struggle with guilt when it comes to their infertility. They ask, "Why is God punishing me this way? Is it because we were intimate before we got married? Is He angry over my brief affair six years ago? Could this be a consequence of my teenage abortion?"

Well, what about it? Could infertility be a result of our behavior? Many writers, including Christians, reject this possibility. They suggest that because God is a God of love, He would never allow sin to result in such a scourge as infertility.

I would like to respectfully and carefully disagree. There is ample evidence that a holy God can and does punish sin. In fact, there is evidence that on at least a couple of occasions God did respond to sin with the affliction of infertility (see Genesis 20:17-18 and 2 Samuel 6:20-23). And what of the person who engages in a promiscuous lifestyle, thereby contracting a sexually transmitted disease that scars the reproductive organs and leads to infertility? While that may not be a personalized punishment, is it not a consequence of sin?

This is not to say that God won't forgive that sin. His forgiveness, available through the redemptive work of Jesus Christ, is real, magnificent, and liberating. "If we confess our sins, he is faithful and just and will forgive us our sins and purify us from all unrighteousness" (1 John 1:9).

Should we then search for some specific shortcoming that explains our infertility? For the vast majority of us, that would be misguided, self-defeating, destructive, and wrong. This is especially true where there is no obvious connection between a sinful behavior and an infertility problem.

Philip Yancey makes an important point about this issue. He notes that when God used suffering as punishment in the Old Testament, it followed His repeated warnings against specific behavior. Yancey observes that punishment is effective only when there is a clear tie between behavior and a warning against that behavior. He writes, "Think of a parent who punishes a young child. It would do little good for that parent to sneak up at odd times during a day and whack that child with no explanation. Such a tactic would produce a neurotic, not an obedient child."[2]

The Bible contains many warnings against making unjustified connections between suffering and sin. Job's friends tried to convince him that he was suffering because he'd sinned, but they were wrong. The disciples of Jesus assumed a certain man was blind because he or his parents had sinned (John 9:1-3), but they were wrong as well. Jesus repeatedly debunked the prevailing opinion that all personal tragedy could be traced to some specific sin.

Even if there is some dark sin in your closet, it does not necessarily follow that infertility is the result. If there were always a correlation between sinfulness and infertility, would abusive mothers be allowed to conceive?

In fact, some of the most righteous people in the Bible suffered from infertility—including Abraham and Sarah, Hannah, and Zechariah and Elizabeth. Regarding the latter, "Both of them were upright in the sight of God, observing all the Lord's commandments and regulations blamelessly" (Luke 1:6).

Countless couples cause themselves unnecessary suffering by assuming their infertility is linked to specific wrongs they've committed. There are other possibilities, and none of them has anything to do with sin.

POSSIBILITY 3: TO TEST OUR FAITH

On Thanksgiving Day last year my sister-in-law announced that she and her husband were trying to have a baby. On Christmas they announced they were pregnant. For them it was a high point in their lives, for me it was a sinking point. As a Christian I had been trusting God, now my faith was being tested as never before.

Can God use trials to test our faith? Absolutely. James 1:2-4 puts it this way: "Consider it pure joy, my brothers, whenever you face trials of many kinds, because you know that the testing of your faith develops perseverance. Perseverance must finish its work so that you may be mature and complete, not lacking anything."

Infertility can be a severe testing of our faith. But why does God test our faith? In his book *When God Doesn't Make Sense,* Dr. James Dobson puts it this way:

> Apparently, most believers are permitted to go through emotional and spiritual valleys that are designed to test their faith in the crucible of fire. Why? Because faith ranks at the top of God's system of priorities. Without it, He said, it is impossible to please Him (Hebrews 11:6). And what is faith? It is the "substance of things hoped for, the evidence of things not seen (Hebrews 11:1, KJV). This determination to believe when the proof is not provided and when the questions are not answered is central to our relationship with the Lord. He will never do anything to destroy the need for faith. In fact, He guides us through times of testing specifically to cultivate that belief and dependence on Him (Hebrews 11:6-7).[3]

I realize that theology alone doesn't heal the deep wounds of infertility or pregnancy loss. The truth is that some of us find our faith crumbling in the crucible of testing. The following was written by one such soul:

> I have totally lost heart. It is hard to pray. It is nearly impossible to read the Bible. I have tried, but I am shocked to discover a

bitter, cynical laugh welling up from my heart when I read the Bible or listen to a sermon. I never anticipated such a huge crisis of my faith.

If your faith seems to be failing, please don't cut yourself off from the very source that can give you strength. Now is the time when you most need the Lord. Tell Him honestly about your feelings; ask Him to increase your faith. Try praying as did the man who asked Jesus to heal his son: "I do believe; help me overcome my unbelief!" (Mark 9:24).

Spend time meditating on God's Word—especially passages in which His people faced great suffering yet kept their faith. Some examples: the Book of Job, Hebrews 11, Psalms 37 and 73, and the story of Shadrach, Meshach, and Abednego (Daniel 3). Allow your soul to be stirred by the words of Habakkuk 3:17-19:

> Though the fig tree does not bud
>   and there are no grapes on the vines,
> though the olive crop fails
>   and the fields produce no food,
> though there are no sheep in the pen
>   and no cattle in the stalls,
> yet I will rejoice in the LORD,
>   I will be joyful in God my Savior.
> The Sovereign LORD is my strength. . . .

Consider reading the following books, too, all of which are available through Christian bookstores: *When God Doesn't Make Sense* by Dr. James Dobson (Tyndale House Publishers, 1993); *Where Is God When It Hurts?* (Zondervan, 1990) and *Disappointment with God* (Harper Paperbacks, 1991), both by Philip Yancey.

POSSIBILITY 4: TO EQUIP US FOR SERVICE

I have so much to learn
And my growth is very slow,
Sometimes I need the mountaintops,
But it's in the valleys I grow.
I do not always understand
Why things happen as they do,
But I am very sure of one thing,
My Lord will see me through.
My little valleys are nothing
When I picture Christ on the cross.
He went through the valley of death;
His victory was Satan's loss.
Forgive me, Lord, for complaining
When I'm feeling so very low,
Just give me a gentle reminder
That it's in the valleys I grow.
Continue to strengthen me, Lord,
And use my life each day
To share Your love with others
And help them find their way.
Thank You for valleys, Lord,
For this one thing I know:
The mountaintops are glorious
But it's in the valleys I grow![4]

Can God use difficult challenges to strengthen us for greater service?
Absolutely!

Consider how Jesus was led into the desert (Matthew 4:1-11). For 40 days, without food and facing the powerful temptations of Satan, He suffered. Meeting that challenge strengthened Him for a three-year marathon of ministry. Later, in Gethsemane (Matthew 26:36-46), He suffered again—and was strengthened to face the much greater agony that would engulf Him the next day on Calvary.

Adversity can help us grow in our relationship to the Lord and in our service to Him. It can turn us toward the only real source of strength, and purifies us as gold is by fire (1 Peter 1:7).

Sylvia and I can testify that our infertility struggle has helped us to grow spiritually. We've grown in our prayer lives, having come to realize how utterly dependent we are on God. We've grown in trusting Him, for we know that the God who has helped us resolve our infertility struggle will help us through the rest of life as well. We've grown in our sensitivity to others' suffering, for we know what it's like to have an empty cradle and wounded hearts.

A woman named Tammy has had a similar experience. She's become, in the words of author Henri Nouwen, a "wounded healer."

After six years of infertility, Tammy faced a decision: She could continue her pity party, or use her hurts to help others. She chose to start an infertility support group. At the first meeting only two women showed up; today new people, including couples, are appearing each time the group meets.

Tammy took her cue in part from 2 Corinthians 1:3-4: "Praise be to the God and Father of our Lord Jesus Christ, the Father of compassion and the God of all comfort, who comforts us in all our troubles, so that we can comfort those in any trouble with the comfort we ourselves have received from God."

As Tammy notes, "When God allowed me to suffer from infertility, He also invested me with a new gift that I did not have before—the gift of compassionate understanding and sensitivity for those who are facing what I have faced."

Marion Powell
Women's Health Information Centre

POSSIBILITY 5: TO GLORIFY GOD

In our trials, God's name can be honored. Jesus named this as a reason for suffering in an incident referred to earlier in this chapter, the healing of a man born blind (John 9:1-3).

When Jesus and His disciples encountered the blind man, they asked Jesus, "Who sinned, this man or his parents, that he was born blind?"

Jesus replied, "Neither this man nor his parents sinned . . . but this happened so that the work of God might be displayed in his life." This man's suffering became a way to reveal God's power, greatness, and compassion.

In the same way, your infertility may be an avenue by which you glorify God.

Could it be that one of your colleagues at work has seen you bear your pain in dignity and trust, and has been moved to seek the God who's given you so much grace?

Have your fellow believers been spurred to praise God as they see your strength in the face of trial?

Or might you, if God blesses you with a child through birth or adoption, be led to glorify and praise Him with greater depth and feeling than if you'd never experienced infertility?

Maybe you'll even be led to start a newsletter or write a book honoring the One who's been there for you in the depths of your pain. God can and does use adversity to bring honor to His name—and the possibilities are endless.

WHERE DO YOU FIT?

At this point you may be wondering, "Where do I fit in? Is my infertility linked to some specific offense? Have I been allowed to suffer because God wants to strengthen me and help me grow? Or does God want to use my suffering to bring honor to Him? How can I know for sure?"

The answer is that most of us may never know for sure why God allowed infertility to be part of our journey. We may want an explanation, thinking that if we knew God's plan the suffering would be easier to take. But most of our "why" questions remain unanswered; the heavens stay silent.

God does not owe us an explanation for the suffering in our lives. Many of us tend to think He does. Following the diving accident in which she was paralyzed, Joni Eareckson Tada felt that way but later changed her mind:

> What a low view of my Master and Creator I had held all these
> years! How could I have dared to assume that almighty God owed
> me explanations? Did I think that because I had done God the
> "favor" of becoming a Christian, He must now check things out
> with me? Was the Lord of the universe under obligation to show me
> how the trials of every human being fit into the tapestry of life?
> Had I never read Deuteronomy 29:29: "There are secrets the Lord
> your God has not revealed to us" (LB)?
>
> What made me think that even if He explained all His ways to
> me I would be able to understand them? It would be like pouring
> million-gallon truths into my one-ounce brain. Why, even the great
> apostle Paul admitted that, though never in despair, he was often
> perplexed (2 Corinthians 4:8).
>
> Hadn't God said, "For as the heavens are higher than the earth,
> so are . . . My thoughts (higher) than your thoughts" (Isaiah 55:9)?
> Didn't one Old Testament author write, "As you do not know the
> path of the wind, or how the body is formed in a mother's womb,
> so you cannot understand the work of God, the maker of all things"
> (Ecclesiastes 11:5, NIV)? In fact, the whole book of Ecclesiastes was
> written to convince people like me that only God holds the keys to
> unlocking the mysteries of life and that He's not loaning them all

out! "He has also set eternity in the hearts of men; yet they cannot fathom what God has done from beginning to end" (Ecclesiastes 3:11, NIV).

If God's mind was small enough for me to understand, He wouldn't be God! How wrong I had been.[5]

I don't think Christians should dwell too long on the "why." It would make little ultimate difference to know the origin of one's infertility problem. We can be sure, though, that whatever God allows the Christian to suffer, He transforms by His divine chemistry into our good and His glory.

God's power to redeem our suffering—whatever its source—is one aspect of the beautiful doctrine of providence. A historic Christian creed summarizes providence in a very personal way when it declares that those who know God may say in faith,

I trust Him so much that I do not doubt He will provide whatever I need for body and soul and He will turn to my good whatever adversity He sends me in this sad world. He is able to do this because He is almighty God; He desires to do this because He is a faithful Father.[6]

9

How Shall We Then Pray?

by John

And because the LORD had closed [Hannah's] womb, her rival kept provoking her in order to irritate her. This went on year after year. Whenever Hannah went up to the house of the LORD, her rival provoked her till she wept and would not eat. Elkanah her husband would say to her, "Hannah, why are you weeping? Why don't you eat? Why are you downhearted? Don't I mean more to you than ten sons?"

. . . In bitterness of soul Hannah wept much and prayed to the LORD . . . saying, "O LORD Almighty, if you will only look upon your servant's misery and remember me, and not forget your servant but give her a son, then I will give him to the LORD for all the days of his life, and no razor will ever be used on his head."

As she kept on praying to the LORD, Eli observed her mouth. Hannah was praying in her heart, and her lips were moving but her voice was not heard. Eli thought she was drunk and said to her,

"How long will you keep on getting drunk? Get rid of your wine."

"Not so, my lord," Hannah replied, "I am a woman who is deeply troubled. I have not been drinking wine or beer; I was pouring out my soul to the LORD." (1 Samuel 1:6-15)

Of all infertility's dimensions, perhaps none is so disturbing as the desolate feeling that others around us simply don't understand. Often we feel alone in our struggle, cut off even from our own spouses.

Hannah must have felt this isolation. Nobody seemed to understand—not her husband, not her rival Peninnah, not even Eli the priest. As one pastor put it, "The human responses to Hannah were almost totally negative. She was surrounded by a taunting rival, a bungling husband, and an insensitive priest."[1]

But Hannah wasn't alone. She poured out her soul to the Lord, the One who always understands.

For Christians facing the turmoil of infertility, there is no resource more important than prayer. Yet prayer raises a multitude of questions, many of which I've been asked over the years:

"How should we pray?"

"Should we pray for healing for our infertility or for submission to God's will?"

"How can I pray when I'm angry with God?"

"Every infertile couple in the Bible eventually received a baby, so if God answered their prayers, why doesn't He answer mine?"

"Is it true that in one way or another God answers every prayer?"

How Should We Pray?

There is no magic formula for prayer, no right or wrong words. All God requires is a real need, a sincere heart, and a simple faith. One statement of faith describes it this way:

Q. How does God want us to pray so that He will listen to us?

A. First, we must pray from the heart to no one other than the one true God. . . .

Second, we must acknowledge our need and misery, hiding nothing, and humble ourselves in His majestic presence.

Third, we must rely on this unshakeable foundation: Even though we don't deserve it, God will surely listen to our prayer because of Christ our Lord. This is what He promised us in His word (Matthew 7:8; John 14:13-14; 16:23; James 1:6).[2]

Hannah's prayer did not contain the well-oiled phrases and pious cliches that plague so many of our prayers. Her plea was from the heart—as ours should be.

Prayer is first of all the honest opening of our heart to God. We need not worry whether this is okay or not. Isn't it true that God knows us inside and out? He sees us as we are and as we feel. Nothing is hidden from His sight. Why not talk to God about everything that fills our heart?[3]

HEALING OR SUBMISSION?

Maybe you can identify with this infertile couple:

We beg and plead with God for children. We pray and delve into why God could possibly be leaving us without more children, and we wonder what He is trying to teach us. Is He teaching us to be patient? Is He telling us to graciously accept the fact that we will never have more children? Right now, we don't have a clue!

Should we pray that God will heal our infertility and grant us our heart's desire for a baby? Or should we pray for the willingness to submit to His will, whatever that may be?

The answer is that we should do both.

Several Bible characters who suffered from infertility prayed earnestly for healing. More than once Abraham made his childless state a matter of prayer (Genesis 15:1-4; 17:18-19). So did Isaac (Genesis 25:21) and Zechariah. When an angel came to tell Zechariah the good news that he and Elizabeth would have a child, the angel said, "Do not be afraid, Zechariah; your prayer has been heard. Your wife Elizabeth will bear you a son . . ." (Luke 1:13).

In each of these situations God blessed with a child those who prayed. This suggests that infertile Christian couples should make their condition a matter of continuing, honest, heartfelt prayer. "The prayer of a righteous man [or woman] is powerful and effective" (James 5:16).

At the same time, believers must always be ready to submit to God's will. That's not in vogue in our culture! The words of the old Frank Sinatra song, "I did it my way," are much more in tune with the spirit of our times. Too many of us are inclined to whisper, "My will, not Thine, be done."

I believe infertility calls us to pray something like this: "Dear God, You know how desperately we want a child. Will You please grant us the desire of our hearts? Will You please give us the laughter of little children? But if not, please give us the willingness to accept Your will, the faith to believe that You still care, and the peace that transcends all understanding as You guard our hearts and minds in Christ Jesus. Amen."

When we ask God for something specific, yet combine that with submission to God's plan, we follow the example of Jesus. With His execution looming only hours away, He made a very specific request: "My Father, if it is possible, may this cup be taken from me." But He added, "Yet not as I will, but as you will" (Matthew 26:39).

This prayer could not have been easy for Jesus. Prayers of submission never are. It takes a huge amount of faith to submit our will to God's. Fortunately, Jesus not only models the way but can give us the strength to follow His lead.

What If I'm Too Angry to Pray?

As noted in the previous chapter, Philip Yancey wrote a book called *Disappointment with God*. I know many Christians suffering from infertility who've gone way beyond disappointment with God; they're angry with Him!

In some cases, they're too angry to pray. As one person relayed to us: "I just don't know how to pray and believe in God anymore. There doesn't seem to be a loving answer for me from a loving God."

Another person wrote, "It is hard to pray. I never anticipated such a huge crisis of my faith. I knew my soul would be crushed when we lost our baby [through miscarriage], but I am beginning to feel as if He has left me."

When we're disappointed or angry with God, it may help to remember that some of the greatest men and women of the Bible had the same experience. Take Moses; God had promised him that the children of Israel would be freed from Egypt. But when Moses went to Pharaoh to declare, "Let my people go," Pharaoh laughed in his face and ordered the Israelites to make bricks without straw.

Was Moses steamed? You bet. Did he tell God about it? Listen to his words: "O LORD, why have you brought trouble upon this people? Is this why you sent me? Ever since I went to Pharaoh to speak in your name, he has brought trouble upon this people, and you have not rescued your people at all" (Exodus 5:22-23).

We might think this is blasphemy, or at least back talk. The amazing thing is that God doesn't seem to mind. There's no hint that He is displeased with Moses.

If you're angry with God, try bringing your anger straight to Him. Tell Him you're angry with Him and why. Don't hold back! He can take it; you won't hurt Him.

Christians often talk about having a personal relationship with God. When Moses took his complaint to the Lord, I believe there was a great deal of personal relationship happening. The same is true for us when we open our hearts to God, even if it's sometimes in anger.

If you find that you simply can't open up to God for a while, find others who'll pray for you. Prayer is like oxygen; we can't survive spiritually for long without it.

IF COUPLES IN THE BIBLE GOT WHAT THEY PRAYED FOR, WHY NOT US?

Why does God have favorites? Do you realize that every woman in the Bible who dealt with infertility eventually got her child? How can I find comfort in Scripture?

—Anonymous

It's true that all the well-known infertile couples in the Bible eventually were able to have children. But it's also true that God does not fulfill every desire. For example, He did not grant His own Son's request that the awful events of Calvary be prevented. And the apostle Paul got a negative answer to repeated requests that his "thorn in the flesh" (probably a physical ailment) be taken away (2 Corinthians 12:7-9).

Yet as Paul understood, God has a positive purpose in everything He does—or does not do—for His children:

But [the Lord] said to me, "My grace is sufficient for you, for my power is made perfect in weakness." Therefore I will boast all the more gladly about my weaknesses, so that Christ's power may rest on me. . . . For when I am weak, then I am strong." (2 Corinthians 12:9-10)

DOES GOD ANSWER EVERY PRAYER?

Yes! Sometimes His answer is "Yes," sometimes "No," and sometimes "Wait." A poem of mine captures this idea:

> When the answer is "Yes,"
> Watch for a blessing coming today.
> When the answer is "No,"
> Trust Him for a better way.
> When the answer is "Wait,"
> Be patient and continue to pray.

God's answer to our prayers may not be what we expect or currently hope. He does things in His way and according to His timetable. So be prepared for answers from unexpected directions and by unexpected means. He is a master at answering prayers in ways that we never anticipate.

Here are two examples:

Dear John and Sylvia,

I am writing to you to thank you for your newsletter. It has been a wonderful resource and it really hit home with me on some tough issues. However, I can joyfully say that I don't need it any longer. This past October my husband and I were overjoyed to give birth to a baby boy. Last Christmas we were resigned to the fact that we were not having children and we gave up pursuing any further infertility treatment. I even signed up for a local support group to deal with my emotions. Early this year we found out that we were pregnant, with no medical help. It was truly a gift from God!

Dear Sylvia,

I am typing this while my two-month-old son sleeps in his bouncy seat. I am still shocked at how he came to be part of our family.

My husband and I had been trying to get pregnant for several years, and we finally decided to try *in vitro*. Unfortunately, after taking the required medication, my estrogen level climbed alarmingly high, and I developed ovarian hyperstimulation syndrome. I passed out several times and was taken by ambulance to the hospital. I recovered, but we left the hospital without a pregnancy.

Later that week my mother-in-law told her friend how sick I had been. That friend said, "That's too bad, but I have a niece who delivered a baby two days ago, and she is planning on releasing her baby for adoption. Is your daughter interested?" That night, the birthmom called and asked if we could come and meet her. Imagine our surprise when we walked in the door, and we were handed a beautiful baby boy, whom we have now adopted.

Pretty amazing, huh?

I encourage you to keep pouring out your soul to the Lord, the One who always understands. And wait for His answer.

10

High-Tech Treatments: Tough Issues

by John

Dear John,

After two surgeries for endometriosis, my doctor has given us little hope of becoming pregnant unless we use IVF-ET [*in vitro* fertilization with embryo transfer]. He thinks I would be an excellent candidate for it, and he is confident it would be successful. My husband and I are holding back because we wonder if this would be honoring to God. What do you think about this?

Louise Brown, the world's first *in vitro* baby, was born July 25, 1978. Newspapers everywhere heralded the event as a great scientific breakthrough. New hope surged for infertile couples. But questions arose as well. IVF was successful, but was it morally acceptable?

Questions about infertility treatment have been around much longer than baby Louise. For decades before her birth, doctors were treating infertility patients through artificial insemination with husband's sperm (AIH) and artificial insemination with donor sperm (DI). Christians struggled, and continue to struggle, with questions:

"Is this okay for Christians?"

"Does the Bible offer any guidelines on Assisted Reproductive Technology (ART)?"

"How do we know what's right or wrong?"

During our own journey of infertility, we were faced with such questions. One day our physician asked, "Have you ever thought about trying artificial insemination?"

The query startled us. "No, we haven't," I finally blurted. "Why?"

"Well," he said after hesitating, "I think that is the logical next step. It can be done with your sperm or with that of a donor."

Suddenly, almost casually, our physician had presented us with an enormous decision. We wanted a baby, but was this an acceptable route to get there? What were the implications, especially of using a donor's sperm? Would this honor God? Was it going a step too far?

Techniques used by today's physicians have advanced far beyond AIH and DI. The range of medical options now runs the gamut from A (artificial insemination) to Z (zygote intrafallopian tube transfer, or ZIFT). With a multitude of options comes a multitude of questions. Which technologies are morally acceptable, and which are not?

There are few resources available that help infertile Christian couples come to grips with these ethical issues. I hope this chapter will help fill that void, enabling you to sort out in a constructive, biblical way some of the most common—and complex—questions.

Q. What kinds of infertility treatments are being used today? There seem to be so many of them, and I'm confused.

A. We asked Dr. William G. Dodds, board-certified reproductive endocrinologist and director of Michigan Reproductive and IVF Center, to provide an overview of today's treatments. Here's what he told us:

Reproductive treatments today fall under two major categories: basic fertility therapy and assisted reproductive technologies.

Basic infertility interventions include use of fertility medications to stimulate egg development. These treatments can be very successful, but increase the risk of multiple pregnancy. Multiple pregnancies—especially higher-order multiple pregnancies (HOM)—are something to avoid because of the danger of preterm labor and birth. Premature infants are at high risk for many problems, including breathing difficulties, digestive abnormalities, intracranial bleeding, impaired mental development, cerebral palsy, and death.

It's important to work closely with your physician when using ovulation induction or fertility medications. The two basic types of fertility medications are clomiphene citrate (also known as Clomid or Serephene) and follicle stimulating hormone (FSH).

Clomiphene citrate (CC) is a synthetic antiestrogen medication. It works to increase the brain's natural FSH level. CC is a pill, generally given daily between menstrual cycle days 3 through 7 or 5 through 9. Both regimens work equally well. Multiple pregnancy risk is about 5 to 10 percent.

FSH medications like Gonal-F, Follistim, and Pergonal have been used for around 40 years to help induce ovulation when CC fails. FSH medications today are given as subcutaneous injections. A patient can easily learn to self-administer FSH.

Usually FSH is started on cycle day 3 and continued for 8 to 12 days. During this time, serial ultrasound and estradiol measurements are made to assess egg development. When the eggs are mature, the patient is given a human chorionic gonadotropin (hCG) injection and will ovulate approximately 36 hours later.

Both of these medications—CC and FSH—can effectively treat many ovulation problems and lead to successful pregnancy.

Newer additions to these medications, used in women with polycystic ovary disease syndrome (PCOS), are insulin-sensitizing agents like metformin (Glucophage), rosiglitazone (Avandia), and pioglitazone (Actos). These agents can help overcome the insulin resistance found in PCOS patients that inhibits normal ovulation. These medications can be effective alone or in conjunction with weight loss. They also can be combined with CC or FSH to help stimulate ovulation.

Then there are the assisted reproductive technologies (ART). They include the following:

1. Intrauterine insemination (IUI)
2. *In vitro* fertilization with embryo transfer (IVF-ET)
3. Gamete intrafallopian tube transfer (GIFT)
4. Zygote intrafallopian tube transfer (ZIFT)

IUI involves washing a sperm specimen so that seminal secretions are separated from the sperm. The sperm are then segregated, generally by centrifuge, to obtain the best, most motile sperm. These are concentrated into a small volume (less than 1 milliliter). The washed sperm can then be inseminated into the female with a catheter that is directed through the cervix and up to the top of the uterus. IUI is done approximately 36 hours after hCG injection, so that sperm arrive around the time of ovulation. IUI can be used in cervical factor, mild male factor, and unexplained infertility cases.

IVF-ET involves four basic steps:

1. Ovulation induction (development of multiple eggs with FSH medications)
2. Egg retrieval
3. *In vitro* fertilization (fertilizing eggs with sperm in a laboratory)
4. Embryo transfer

The egg retrieval step is done under vaginal ultrasound guidance. The patient is given IV sedation and pain medication; a needle aligned with a vaginal ultrasound is guided through the top of the vagina to the ovary. Eggs are then aspirated into a test tube and fertilized in the laboratory.

If there is a male factor, a technique known as intracytoplasmic sperm insertion (ICSI) is done to introduce a single sperm into each egg. Two to five days after egg retrieval, embryos can be transferred back to the patient.

In IVF, embryo transfer is to the uterus—using a soft catheter inserted through the cervix. In ZIFT, early stage embryos are transferred to the fallopian tubes one to two days after fertilization. This is accomplished by doing a laparoscopy and inserting the embryo into the fallopian tubes.

GIFT, on the other hand, involves three steps:
1. Ovulation induction (as in IVF and ZIFT)
2. Laparoscopic egg retrieval
3. Laparoscopic transfer of eggs and sperm to the fallopian tubes

GIFT procedures are not performed often anymore. Today reproductive endocrinologists feel it's best to first fertilize the egg to better control the number of embryos that are returned to the patient.

Comparing IVF to ZIFT, the consensus is that they are generally equal in terms of pregnancy success. Some studies have suggested ZIFT is more successful, and may be most applicable when combined with a diagnostic laparoscopy or in patients in whom transcervical embryo transfer is difficult.

It's important when contemplating these procedures to carefully follow appropriate guidelines for the number of embryos to transfer back. The American Society of Reproductive Medicine (ASRM) has established guidelines primarily based on patient age, since multiple pregnancy risk decreases with age.

It's also important to check the quality of the program you plan to use. Its success rate can be obtained from the Centers for Disease Control at www.cdc.gov/nccdphp/drh/art.htm.

Q. Is artificial insemination with a husband's sperm okay?

A. In artificial insemination using a husband's sperm (AIH), the sperm is collected by means of masturbation and inserted through a tube (rather than by intercourse) into the vagina. Intrauterine insemination (IUI) is an adaptation of this technique.

There is a wide range of viewpoints on artificial insemination, even when strictly limited to using the husband's sperm. The Roman Catholic Church has strong objections to the practice. The official teachings of the church argue that the unitive and procreative aspects of sex must be inseparably linked. Technology that seems to replace normal sex tends to be viewed as illegitimate in official Catholic doctrine.

Nevertheless, there are numerous Roman Catholic theologians who disagree. They argue that marriage partners express their love regularly by intercourse, which they would render fertile if they could. But since they can't, they may use an artificial process to achieve their legitimate purpose. Following this reasoning, many Roman Catholic couples are convinced they may pursue AIH without violating their consciences or their faith.

Evangelical Christians are generally more open to the use of AIH. Personally, I do not believe there is anything morally wrong with the procedure. Sylvia and I pursued this course of treatment for our infertility, though unsuccessfully. It was not a particularly pleasant experience, but I never felt it was immoral.

I agree that sex, love, and procreation belong together. Where this does not achieve a pregnancy, I can see no valid objection to AIH. I do not view the procedure as a separation of the couple's unity, but as a result of it. In

AIH the child is conceived as the fruit of the union between a man and his wife; the artificial means merely assist the natural process.

Q. My husband's sperm count and motility levels are low. Our physician is recommending the use of donor sperm. Is this morally acceptable?

A. Some Christians have insisted that using donor sperm or eggs constitutes adultery. I strongly disagree.

Adultery involves an act of intercourse, or at least lustful desire (Matthew 5:28). Using donor eggs or sperm does not involve either.

A more serious objection is that using donor sperm or eggs involves a third party in the process of having a baby—though in a non-sexual, non-adulterous way. Opponents of this procedure argue that the "one flesh" concept of marriage precludes the intrusion of a third person's genetic material and history.

For that reason some organizations like Focus on the Family and Bethany Christian Services do not support using donor sperm or eggs. In his *Complete Marriage and Family Home Reference Guide*, Dr. James Dobson explains:

> . . . I am strongly opposed to the practice of creating fertilized eggs from "donors" outside the immediate family (this would include the donation of sperm or eggs from a brother or sister of the husband and wife wishing to conceive). In my opinion, to engage in such activity would be to "play God"—to create human life outside the bonds of marriage.[1]

Some Christian writers and physicians do not oppose the practice. Still others do not take a clear position regarding donor insemination. This wide gamut of opinions makes it difficult for believers who are facing very real ethical questions.

Christian authors Sandra Glahn and William Cutrer suggest that there is no simple right or wrong answer to the question of whether it is morally acceptable to use a donor: "We do not believe the answer to be a simple yes or no. We must seek scriptural guidelines and then prayerfully, depending on the Holy Spirit's guidance, draw a conclusion that is, for us, gracious and sound."[2]

What would Sylvia and I do if we were still in the midst of our infertility struggle, and our physician recommended using donor sperm? Would we feel comfortable going that route?

In all honesty, I don't think so. For me it would be psychologically difficult to accept the fact that my wife was impregnated with another man's sperm. For both of us it would be morally difficult to accept the involvement of a third identity in our marriage, though anonymously and sexlessly.

If you are thinking about using donor sperm or eggs, I encourage you to carefully consider the ethical issues. Too often desperate couples plunge into the world of high-tech treatments without weighing the implications. Consult an informed pastor if possible; pray for wisdom.

Consider, too, the future well-being of your child. Don't just weigh the impact that using a donor might have on you and your spouse. One of the most important tasks of childhood is to answer the question "Who am I?" For children born through the means of a donor, an important part of their story is missing. Unlike those involved in open adoption (see chapter 14), most sperm donors are guaranteed anonymity. Since it's so important for a youngster to understand his or her identity, should couples conceive a child for whom one biological parent remains unknowable?

In a 1995 letter written to *Stepping Stones*, Dr. James Dobson advised couples to pray the following before utilizing any form of ART: "Lord, we want to do Your will in this regard. We will be listening for Your voice in the weeks ahead. Please speak to us through the means You prefer. And when we have understood You, we will obey."

Q. My wife isn't ovulating properly, so our doctor is recommending Clomid. We've read that using fertility drugs can lead to multiple pregnancies, and we're concerned about the moral implications. What's your view on this?

A. Many couples are so intent on having a baby that they never consider the possibility of ending up with too many. As one doctor put it, "Patients don't hear what physicians tell them about the risk of multiple pregnancy. They don't hear a doctor say there may be too many, because they are so focused on not having any!"

I don't believe it's morally wrong to use fertility drugs. But as Dr. Dodds noted earlier in this chapter, there is a small but real risk of multiple pregnancies with certain medications. Couples should ask themselves, "How would we accept the news that we're pregnant with triplets? Quadruplets? Or even septuplets?"

In the case of higher-order multiple pregnancies, some physicians urge selective termination—abortion—of the weakest fetus(es) in order to provide the best chance that the remaining babies will be born healthy. Such physicians argue that three healthy babies are better than four who are born prematurely, have a low birth weight, and face the potential of lifelong complications.

As a pro-life Christian, I believe abortion is permissible only to save the life of the mother. Even if you share that view, however, be forewarned that such a commitment is easier in the abstract than when you're faced with a risky, real-life multiple pregnancy.

Many Christian couples, with carefully prescribed dosages and a competent physician, are willing to take a limited risk. To help you decide, sit down with your physician before proceeding with any fertility medication and ask questions like these:

• What are the side effects of this medication?

• What are the risks of multiple pregnancy with this medication?

• Are there medications or dosages that limit the risk of multiple pregnancy?

• If a multiple pregnancy does happen, do you (the physician) ever recommend selective termination? Will you honor our commitment to carry all pregnancies to term?

Q. It looks like the next logical step for us is IVF-ET using my sperm and my wife's eggs. How do you feel about this procedure from a Christian perspective?

A. As Dr. Dodds has noted in this chapter, *in vitro* fertilization with embryo transfer involves giving a woman a combination of drugs to produce multiple eggs, which are then retrieved using a needle guided by ultrasound. The number of eggs retrieved varies, but eight to 12 is fairly typical. Each healthy-looking, mature egg is fertilized.

After a few days the physician selects three to six of the most promising-looking embryos and implants them in the uterus where, hopefully, pregnancy will result. Since the success rate is only about 50 percent for each IVF attempt—and that's at the best clinics—unused embryos are usually frozen (cryopreserved) for possible later attempts.

As one who believes that life begins when an egg is fertilized, I'm convinced that every embryo created in the IVF process must be respected and treated as human life. As Horton the Elephant says so well in the Dr. Seuss book *Horton Hatches the Egg*, "A person's a person no matter how small."

If each embryo is recognized as human life, there is a host of moral concerns that couples should face before agreeing to an IVF procedure. For example, suppose your physician retrieves 12 eggs, 10 of which are healthy and mature. They are fertilized, and at least eight embryos begin growing. Your doctor then implants three or four of those embryos in your womb, hoping at least one of them will "take." The remaining four or five are frozen for potential later attempts.

What happens if the initial try is successful and you're blessed with a baby—or two or three? What about the embryos you've allowed to be frozen?

Or what if one partner dies before the frozen embryos can be used? What if you and your spouse get a divorce, or decide not to have children after all?

Consider the dilemma of a couple we'll call Joe and Sally. On the urging of their physician, and without fully realizing the implications, they agreed to have multiple eggs fertilized for implantation in Sally's uterus. Since not all the embryos could be implanted initially, the rest were frozen for later attempts.

Surprise! Joe and Sally are now expecting triplets. They're ecstatic but frantic. What do they do with the human lives they have "on ice"? The doctor wants to destroy the unneeded embryos, and Joe and Sally are quite sure that three children will give them a full quiver.

Because of complications like these, some Christian couples are insisting that no more than three or four eggs are fertilized, and that all of the resulting embryos be implanted in the womb. In other words, no unused embryos will be frozen for later attempts. Such couples also insist that there will be no selective reduction, and that they will receive all resulting pregnancies as a gift from God.

This is a life-honoring approach. Be aware, though, that not all physicians will agree to these stipulations. Since retrieving eggs is the most difficult, painful, and expensive part of any IVF procedure, some doctors argue that it would be a shame to throw away eggs that are not being used. The time to settle this issue is before the procedure takes place.

There is also the question of cost. At this writing, the price of an IVF attempt ranges from $4,000 to $10,000. In the U.S., 13 states currently require insurance companies to cover high-tech treatments like IVF—but in the remaining states most insurance companies will *not* cover the costs.

That raises moral questions for many Christian couples: "Can we reasonably afford to spend thousands of dollars for an IVF procedure? Would it be exercising good stewardship of our resources? Since the results of an IVF procedure aren't certain, should we risk this much money? If IVF fails, will we have enough resources to consider adoption?"

I'm not trying to talk anyone out of using IVF-ET. I simply want couples to reflect on the implications of this procedure before plunging forward.

The fact is that many Christians have enjoyed the benefits of parenthood by means of IVF. The following is a case in point:

> I have struggled with infertility for the past four years. Each month
> was an emotional roller coaster, but your newsletter always managed
> to come when I was feeling my lowest. They . . . reminded me that
> God was in control of my life (not me), and He did have a plan for
> my husband and me. After our second try at IVF, we were blessed
> to hear the good news that we were pregnant. I am 19 weeks along
> now and expect our baby in December. Praise the Lord!

Q. We've agreed to undergo an IUI. Do you have any ethical concerns about this procedure?

A. In an IUI (intrauterine insemination) the sperm are washed and the most active selected via a centrifuge. These are introduced into the uterus where, it is hoped, one of them will unite with an egg produced by the female. When this is done using a husband's sperm and a wife's egg, I have no ethical qualms about the procedure. If a donor is involved, the same concerns raised earlier come into play.

Q. What about ZIFT?

A. For those who believe life begins at conception, ZIFT and ICSI raise the same moral questions as IVF-ET. For some, GIFT is more acceptable—since fertilization takes place within the body rather than *in vitro*. I believe these procedures can be used by a Christian couple without moral complications—assuming the sperm and eggs come from the couple and that they have a careful, life-honoring plan for all the embryos that are created.

Q. What about the idea of "adopting" frozen embryos remaining from someone else's IVF procedure?

A. In *Complete Marriage and Family Home Reference Guide*, Dr. James Dobson includes this question from a woman considering *in vitro* fertilization:

> Our doctor has access to fertilized eggs that will be destroyed if they aren't implanted in a recipient woman. A couple whom we don't know had their eggs frozen for future use but decided not to use them. How do you think God would view our accepting the eggs and giving life to one of them? Can you tell me whether or not it is right to "create" a child in this way?

Here's part of Dr. Dobson's answer:

> Your acceptance of [these embryos] would provide an opportunity for life for at least one embryo that presumably would otherwise be destroyed. . . . I believe this procedure is quite different than an infertile couple seeking out an egg or sperm donor, which, as I indicated, is creating life from outside the family.
> I would tend to see the option you've been offered as "adoption"

at an earlier stage of development. . . . From a theological stand-
point, I believe the fertilized eggs in question already have an eternal
soul (which occurred at the moment of fertilization). Most important, you and your husband had nothing to do with the decision to
fertilize the eggs. By implanting them, you would merely be rescu-
ing embryos that have no other possibility of life.

I have discussed this idea at some length with Dr. Joe McIlhaney, a gynecologist and infertility specialist. . . . We would recommend considering the adoption of the eggs only after serious prayer
and consideration of the following points: (a) Make sure the potential donors have been screened for HIV, sexually transmitted dis-
eases, and other health facts; (b) insist that your physician thaw only
one to three living embryos (some embryos do not survive the
thawing process). We recommend no more than three embryos be
implanted because of the risk of multiple pregnancy; (c) insert all
living embryos and be prepared to accept the possibility of twins or
triplets if that is what happens; and (d) an attorney should handle
the relinquishing of rights by the donor couple and the formal
adoption process, etc. (The legal climate concerning this procedure
is not settled, so it would be wise to secure legal counsel familiar
with these issues.)[3]

In legal terms, there is technically no such thing as "embryo adoption." In the eyes of the law embryos are not considered persons; their
status is regulated by contract law, not adoption law. To transfer embryos
from one set of parents to another, both couples sign a carefully worded
contract spelling out terms of the transfer. Laws are beginning to catch
up with practice, however, and in five states there are laws specifically
governing embryo donation.

One organization dealing with this issue is Nightlight Christian
Adoptions. Its embryo adoption program is called Snowflakes. Why?

Because each embryo is a beautiful, unique, fragile creation of God. As Ron Stoddart, founder of the Snowflakes program, has said, "An embryo is not a potential human life—it is a human life with potential."

Embryo adoption does not come without implications and complications. Those who donate embryos must reckon with the fact that their genetic offspring are being given to others to be raised by them. Those who adopt need to provide the resulting children with full, age-appropriate disclosure about the nature of their birth.

Nevertheless, embryo adoption can be an answer to prayer. As one recipient of such a gift says, "To have someone say, 'They are from us, but they are for you,' is the most awesome thing."

For more information, contact:

Nightlight Christian Adoptions
801 E. Chapman Ave., Suite 106
Fullerton, CA 92831
Phone: (714) 278-1020
www.snowflakes.org

Q. What about surrogate mothers? Is that a valid option for Christians?

A. The cover story of *People* magazine, March 10, 2003, was titled, "She's Having My Babies." Though she already had three grown children, former *Good Morning America* host Joan Lunden, 52, turned to the Center for Surrogate Parenting in Encino, California. The Center linked Joan and her husband with Deborah Bolig, 42, who for a fee of approximately $22,000 became a surrogate mother of twins. From all appearances, it was a happy experience both for the surrogate mother and the new parents.

Is this a solution for believers? Generally speaking, I don't encourage Christians to consider this option. Here's why:

• As in the case of using a donor for sperm or eggs, surrogate motherhood raises many of the concerns already addressed in this chapter.

• A surrogate may begin to view the baby she is bearing as hers. A woman who voluntarily relinquishes a child, as in adoption, does so after the baby is born. In a surrogate situation, a woman is to relinquish a child before that child is even conceived. Can we rightfully ask this of a surrogate?

• In most agreements with a surrogate, there is a commercial element. In essence, a woman agrees to "rent" her womb for a fee. This appears to be tantamount to selling (or renting) one's body for commercial gain. I don't believe this is honoring to God.

• Surrogacy can be exorbitantly expensive. In the article just cited, Joan Lunden and her husband indicated that the whole process cost $65,000. Is it wise stewardship to spend that much money to have a baby in this manner?

Those considering "altruistic surrogacy," in which the surrogate is not paid but carries the baby for a friend or relative as an act of love, need to consider the implications. Moral objections might be overcome if there were no payment involved, if the husband and wife (not donors) provided the sperm and eggs, if all spouses fully supported the endeavor, and if a legal agreement spelled out the obligations of all parties and provided for unforeseen contingencies.

But there would still be risks. What happens if the sister or friend who is carrying your baby develops extremely high blood pressure, and the doctor says her health will be compromised if she continues the pregnancy? What if the surrogate is driving and causes an accident that results in permanent brain injury or even death to your unborn child? If the baby is born prematurely and needs an extended stay in the hospital's neonatal intensive care unit, who will be responsible for the medical bills?

Many potential problems could be addressed in a carefully written agreement between the two couples involved. But it's virtually impossible for any agreement to cover every possible contingency.

Q. With all the babies available for adoption, is it wrong for us to continue medical treatment in the hope of having biological children?

A. It's natural for couples to long for a child born from their love. A pastor has described this desire well:

> If [spouses find] themselves longing and praying for a child, there is nothing wrong in wanting that child to be flesh of their flesh, bone of their bone, image of their own genetic blueprints. Is this not what God himself prized when he created us? He made us in his own image. And do not all of the living things he created carry within themselves the power to reproduce "according to their kinds"?
>
> Notice what we first look for in a baby: which parent they resemble. The longing to have a child that is genetically our very own is woven deeply into the fabric of most couples' lives. So for a couple to embark on a quest to have their own biological child, even at some risk and significant cost, is not only understandable but, I would contend, good and right. It is neither sinful or selfish.[4]

Would it be better to adopt than to pursue high-tech treatments? Each couple needs to prayerfully examine its reasons for preferring one option to the other, and to consider its opportunities. You may find chapter 14 of this book helpful in that regard. Adoption is a wonderful option for many, yet there is no need to feel guilty about the desire to have a biological child.

THE CHOICES ARE YOURS

Using today's medical technology to have a baby raises complicated, soul-searching questions for Christians. If you face these difficult decisions, my heart goes out to you.

My hope and prayer is that the information you've just read will help you make God-honoring decisions as you learn to seek His will.

> Trust in the LORD with all your heart
> and lean not on your own understanding;
> in all your ways acknowledge him,
> and he will make your paths straight.
>
> Proverbs 3:5-6

11

Pregnancy Loss and Infant Death

by John and Sylvia

The wind whipped through my hair as I slowly emerged from the car. Small raindrops speckled my body, and I could feel my socks become damp through my sandals as we slowly walked to the graveside. As we gazed at the grave, I pulled my coat tighter hoping to gather some warmth.

The bleakness of the moment echoed throughout the silent cemetery. As I watched the roses being set down, a ray of sunlight pierced through the heavy clouds and shone briefly on the grave where our three babies were buried. . . . Instead of feeling peace from this sign of hope, I felt intense anger. Who wanted a ray of sunlight when our three babies had been so cruelly taken from us? Even the barren trees surrounding the cemetery had more hope than we did. They knew life was arriving in the spring. I felt no hope. My life was over, and God had disappeared.

Yesterday was the memorial service for our three children who, one by one, died shortly after birth. How would we survive? God had ignored the thousands of prayers begging for even one of their lives. God was now ignoring our pain and us. Where was He? When I was younger I always thought He answered prayers and loved me. How foolish I had been!

After the death of our babies, going into the real world only brought pain and grief. Any mention of children would set me back, and depression would set in. I just wanted to return to my bed and curl up into a tight ball.

My quiet times each morning helped me counter the lows of the previous day. Unfortunately, my husband, Doug, never had the mornings to nurse his wounds. One Sunday he informed me he dreaded attending church. Seeing all the children and hearing the kids' announcements was too painful. After quietly thanking God for my strength that morning, I assured Doug that we would feel joy again. While earthly happiness is elusive, joy is eternal contentment. We'd be with our babies in eternity and experience more joy than we could imagine—we needed to hang on to that peace![1]

The preceding account was written by Jackie Roskamp. After years of trying to become parents, Jackie and her husband, Doug, were overjoyed to experience a pregnancy—triplets, no less!

All too soon, however, the joy turned to worry. Jackie experienced a troubled pregnancy. Finally worry was replaced by heartrending sorrow as the babies were born too prematurely to survive.

COMMON THREADS

Jackie and her husband are certainly not the only ones to celebrate the joy of a pregnancy, only to suffer heartbreak. In the United States, for example, an estimated 600,000 women experience pregnancy loss or infant death each year.

While each loss is unique, there are common threads in the stories of those who endure the death of an unborn or newborn child. If you've faced such a loss and have experienced one or more of the following, it may help to know that you're not alone.

1. *Spiritual doubt and confusion.* The question of why God allowed this to happen takes a cruel turn. Couples who never become pregnant often find a "Why?" escaping through clenched teeth, but those who are blessed with a pregnancy, only to lose their baby, face an added sense of bewilderment:

> I am so confused. WHY? Why did I get pregnant after all that we have been through only to lose our twins through miscarriage? God could have prevented the pregnancy or made one of our babies healthy. So I am trying to figure out what He is saying to me. Is He trying to say, "Do not waste any more money on IVF," or "All your babies will be unhealthy," or is this supposed to build my character? (If so, I am failing.) I don't know where to look for answers.

2. *A continuing sense of loss.* Those who've never personally collided with pregnancy loss or infant death often assume that those who have soon heal and resume their lives. But it's common to face a continuing sense of loss for a long time:

> Not a week goes by without my thinking about how old one of my children would be, or what my life would be like if one or more of them were here with me now. My arms still ache to hold each baby. . . . I saw the beating heart on the ultrasound . . . I felt the bulge in my abdomen . . . I held the last tiny baby in my hand, saw his blue eyes, counted his fingers and toes.

3. *A feeling of emptiness, isolation, and distance.* It's not unusual for those who've experienced miscarriage or infant loss to feel empty and emotionally distant from those around them.

"Why do I have this empty feeling in the pit of my stomach?" one woman asks.

Another says, "My best friend and I used to be so close. Now it seems as if she doesn't really understand me. It's creating a problem."

4. *Wondering what the child would have been like.* It's natural to wonder what a daughter or son would have been like had she or he lived. Kristin Siebers expresses it well:

> Dear little one,
> I never saw you with my eyes,
> But I saw you with my heart.
> From the moment I knew of you,
> I loved you.
> I wondered what you would be like:
> Would you have your daddy's big eyelashes?
> My smile?
> His big, bright eyes?
> My musical gifts?
> His ability to play the drums?
> We planned to teach you about Jesus.
> But He took you in His arms
> Before you could reach ours.[2]

5. *Comfortless comments from others.* It's hard to find solace in statements like, "There was probably something wrong with the baby, so things are better off this way." The same is true of "You can always try again," which seems to imply that a child born in the future could replace the one who was lost.

Someone has suggested that any comment beginning with "at least" is likely to be unhelpful. For example: "At least it happened before the baby was born," or "At least you got pregnant once." Those who make such comments may be trying to help, but those who grieve find the words are superficial and trivialize the loss.

6. *Anxiety during future pregnancies.* For most couples, becoming pregnant is a joyful event filled with hope and celebration. For couples who have endured the trauma of one or more pregnancy losses, "expecting" brings as much fear as happiness:

> My miscarriage has robbed me of the joy of this pregnancy. Every ultrasound appointment fills me with dread. What if they can't find my baby's heartbeat? Each morning when I wake up, I worry. Will I feel my baby move today? Our friends, who are also pregnant, are excitedly fixing up the baby's room, picking out clothes, and buying a crib, but I don't want to do any of those things for fear that my baby might not live.

Some couples are afraid to tell others they've become pregnant again. As one woman confided, "I don't want to tell anyone that I am pregnant again; I could not stand the pain of telling them that something happened."

7. *Tension in the marriage.* The following reactions are common among women: "Does my husband feel as badly as I do about our baby? Does he know that since our baby died, I hate having sex? Why do I feel so unattractive? Why is becoming pregnant again such an obsession for me, but not for him?"

Conversely, it's not uncommon for the husband to think, "I have to be strong for my wife's sake. She'll only grieve more if I show my emotions, so I'll keep my thoughts to myself. Why has she withdrawn sex? Is she blaming me? I know she wants to become pregnant again, but I'm afraid of what losing another baby would do to her. It seems like she's crying all the time, and it's really getting to me. I wish we could be happy again, like we were before the baby died."

8. *Longing for a heavenly reunion.* A recurring theme among Christian couples is confidence that they'll see their babies again. They find tremendous comfort in knowing that their little ones are safe in the arms of Jesus, and that one day there will be a glorious reunion:

> We will miss your first smile, your first word and cry,
> We know you're with Jesus, and one day we'll know "Why?"
> Our precious angel baby, safe and without harm,
> We'll see you again someday and wrap you in our loving arms.[3]

HEALING WITH HOPE

There is no easy way to walk the road of pregnancy-related loss. Yet there are ways to lessen the pain and promote the healing process. Here are some suggestions.

1. *Grieve in your own way.* Greg Bodin, director of pastoral care at North Memorial Medical Center in Robbinsdale, Minnesota, has worked with hundreds of families who've experienced miscarriage, stillbirth, or early infant death. He and his wife have also suffered the loss of two children through miscarriage and stillbirth. Among the things he's learned are these:

• Loss is uniquely personal. There is no typical response or "right" reaction to a pregnancy loss or death of a newborn.

• Feel the freedom to grieve in your own way. Don't let anyone prescribe how you should feel, and don't try to adapt your feelings to the expectations of others.

• Remember that the length of pregnancy doesn't correlate to the grief felt. Some parents experience a great sense of loss even though the pregnancy was short-term.

2. *Personalize your baby.* It's helpful in the long run to acknowledge your baby's personal identity. Name the baby, find out his or her sex, and hold him or her if possible. Bereavement services coordinator Nancy Kingma gives the following advice:

> If the parent does not attach to the lost baby, they cannot detach. Parents can attach to the baby by seeing, holding, and touching their baby. I encourage and support the parents in seeing the results of the pregnancy loss, even if the baby is very tiny. This is particularly important because others will minimize the loss and make it seem as if it was not real or important. I also encourage parents to create a memory box in which they can place valued items such as [photographs] and/or ultrasound pictures of their baby, footprints, locks of hair, or a baby bracelet. Some parents write a poem that commemorates their lost child. Others find it healing to write a journal of their feelings. All of these items validate their baby and help the parents to know that this baby was a real and precious person. By all means, ask your pastor to hold a memorial service for your baby—even if it is a small service with just a few of your most precious family and friends present.[4]

3. *Don't rush.* Others may encourage you to "move on" before you're ready. You and your spouse need to accomplish the work of grieving first. This includes the following:

• Accepting the reality of the loss, that the person who was taken from you is gone and is not coming back.

• Facing rather than escaping or denying the pain.

• Adjusting to a routine which does not include your missing baby.

• Redirecting your emotional energy from dwelling on your loss to other productive areas.

All of this takes time. For many there is no "magic moment" when the decision is made to move on. Indeed, some sense of loss will last for a lifetime. But sooner or later the life-dominating, all-consuming grief that parents experience at the moment of loss will give way to a renewed interest in the joy of living.

If you find yourself "stuck" at some point in the grieving process, don't hesitate to consult a trained counselor. Anger and depression are often encountered on this journey, but they need not be long-term companions.

4. *Bring your turmoil to God.* You won't be the first believer who's raised anguished, even angry, cries to the Lord, nor will you be the last.

Don't be afraid that He'll get angry with you for being honest about how you feel. Pour out your heart to the Lord. He understands. He listens. He cares. "As a father has compassion on his children, so the LORD has compassion on those who fear him; for he knows how we are formed, he remembers that we are dust" (Psalm 103:13-14).

5. *Find someone who cares for you in a way that helps you.* This might not be easy; many may care, but few may be equipped to help. Most couples who suffer loss are not particularly aided by those who quote a lot of Bible verses, leave a stack of literature to read, or overemphasize tomorrow's hope as a way of erasing today's pain. Rather, it is most helpful to find people who . . .

• listen a lot and speak little.

• let you ask tough questions without thinking they need to have all the answers.

• allow you to express real feelings without becoming uncomfortable.

• touch, embrace, and share tears.

• are available—not only days after the event, but weeks and months later.

• understand that certain milestones, such as an expected due date or first anniversary of the loss, may be especially difficult days on which you need support.

• recognize that your feelings are unpredictable—that there may be some days when you feel like talking about it, and other days when you don't want to think about it.

Try to find at least one loving Christian caregiver like this. If you do, you'll be taking a giant step on your journey toward healing and hope.

A LIST OF HELPS

The following resources and ministries specialize in helping couples cope with pregnancy loss, stillbirth, and infant death.

Grieving the Child I Never Knew by Kathe Wunnenberg (Zondervan, 2001)
This is an excellent devotional guide for finding comfort after the loss of an unborn or newborn child.

Empty Arms: Hope and Support for Those Who Have Suffered a Miscarriage, Stillbirth, or Tubal Pregnancy by Pam Vredevelt (Multnomah Publishers, 2001)
Written by a licensed counselor who knows from personal experience what it means to suffer a pregnancy loss, this book offers comfort, practical wisdom, and hope.

From Sorrow to Serenity by Susan Fletcher (Hunter House Publications, 1998)
This book guides the reader through Scripture and thought-provoking meditations on the loss of an unborn or newborn child. Writing from her own experience, the author shares insights on hope, healing, and peace.

M.E.N.D. (Mommies Enduring Neonatal Death)
This nonprofit Christian organization reaches out to those who've lost a child to miscarriage, stillbirth, or infant death, and offers a way to share experiences through a bimonthly newsletter and Web site.

www.mend.org
P.O. Box 1007
Coppell, TX 75019
Phone: (888) 695-MEND

I Can't Find a Heartbeat: Hope and Help for Those Who Have Lost an Unborn Child by Melissa Sexson Hanson (Review and Herald Publishing Association, 1999)

For those who have lost an unborn child, this book addresses such topics as "What is God's perspective on the unborn? What does the Bible say about death? How can we trust God after a tragedy?"

A Place to Remember

This publishing company produces a variety of helpful resources for those who've been touched by a crisis in pregnancy or the death of a baby. Some of the resources are Bible-based; some are not. For a free booklet, e-mail aptr@aplacetoremember.com or call (800) 631-0973.

www.aplacetoremember.com
1885 University Avenue, Suite 110
Saint Paul, MN 55104

12

Secondary Infertility: A Misunderstood Pain

by John and Sylvia

Christmas vacations were sometimes not much fun," recalls Delores, "especially on snowy days when I could not go out to play." As an only child, Delores felt lonely without a sibling to play hide-and-seek or "let's pretend" games.

Dolores didn't like being an only child. Now she desperately wants a sibling for her four-year-old son. "My husband grew up with two brothers," she explains, "and they still all have a great time together. I want that level of closeness for my son."

That son is also pressuring Delores. "When are you going to get a new baby?" he keeps asking. "I want a little brother to play with."

After her son was born, Delores was able to conceive once. But that ended in an early miscarriage. "If it takes much longer to have another baby," Delores says with a sigh, "our son will be too old to be a playmate."

Delores and her husband are among the ranks of those who suffer from secondary infertility—a condition defined as the inability to have another child after conceiving and giving birth at least once.

While the precise numbers aren't known, it's estimated that more women suffer from secondary infertility than from primary infertility. This estimate is based on the fact that a woman's most fertile years are under age 25, and many of those experiencing secondary infertility are 25 or older.

If you're experiencing secondary infertility, most of the preceding chapters apply to you. But you face additional challenges. Some of the most common questions raised by secondary infertility follow, along with our responses. We hope you find them helpful.

Q. If I have one child, I can't really be infertile, can I?

A. Yes. Infertility is defined as the inability to conceive a child, or to carry a child to a live birth, after one or more years of normal sexual relations. This includes those who have one or more children, but are unable to have the additional children they desire.

A couple may have two children and deeply desire a third or even a fourth to complete its family circle. As someone once told us, "When the desire for a child is there, it is there—whether you already have one child or two or three."

If your longing for another child is not being fulfilled, and this is putting a strain on your emotional, relational, and spiritual health, it's time to be honest. You may be facing secondary infertility.

Q. Why do I feel so guilty about wanting another child?

A. This is normal. Perhaps you say to yourself, "Why am I so desperate to have another child? Why isn't one enough for me? Does God think I'm ungrateful for the child He's already given us? I'm angry at myself for feeling so sad."

Remember that you're experiencing the loss of an important hope. Consider this: A couple blessed with five or six children will mourn if even one of those children dies. Will anyone suggest that those parents have no right to feel sad, since they still have other children?

Similarly, when a husband and wife are unable to have an additional child, it represents the death of one of their most significant life goals. It is painful.

For couples making their way through the valley of secondary infertility, guilt is normal—but unnecessary.

Q. Why doesn't anyone understand?

A. Those who suffer from primary infertility encounter plenty of misunderstanding. This can be even more true of those afflicted by secondary infertility. They may hear many "at least" comments—"At least you have one," or "At least you got pregnant once, so it's bound to happen again."

Even some of those experiencing primary infertility demonstrate little empathy for those who have one child but want another. As Alice Domar, past president of the Mental Health Professional Group of the American Society for Reproductive Medicine, says, "Secondary infertility patients can't even count on support from those with primary infertility." When Domar puts together a course geared toward helping infertile women cope, she can include only one or two with secondary infertility. Some of the primary patients, she says, "can't stand" having them around.[1]

Those with secondary infertility stand somewhere between the world of fertility and the world of the empty cradle. As Debra Bridwell puts it, they are "part of the parent 'club,' if only on the fringe."[2]

What can couples with secondary infertility do? We encourage them to establish relationships with others who are undergoing a similar struggle. An excellent resource is Hannah's Prayer at www.hannah.org. This organization maintains an e-mail network specifically for those with secondary infertility. Stepping Stones offers a discussion forum for those with this problem, at http://stepforums.bethany.org.

We also urge those struggling with primary infertility not to dismiss the pain of those who have at least one child. Take seriously the words of Debra Bridwell: "Try to relate to secondary infertile women as you would wish others to relate to your infertility."[3]

Q. Are there other challenges associated with secondary infertility?

A. Absolutely! Not only do you have to face the physical and emotional strains of infertility treatment, but you must do so while raising a child. Among other things, that may mean having to find a baby-sitter during those inconvenient appointments with your physician or lab.

Then there are questions from the child(ren) you already have. It's not always easy to answer that innocent but painful query, "Mommy, Daddy, when am I going to have a new baby brother or sister?"

Finances can be an additional source of stress. Those being treated for primary infertility can face huge financial burdens, but in some cases may be able to take a monetary leap of faith that a couple with one or more children can't.

Q. What do we tell those who ask if we're planning to have another child?

A. It helps to prepare an answer, one that you and your spouse agree upon. One woman, Jennifer, writes that she and her husband respond this way: "We don't seem to be able to have any more children, but we trust God's plan for our family."

If you're comfortable with it, this is an excellent answer. It shares your struggle with infertility—and shares your faith.

When you and your spouse decide what you're going to say, try role-playing your responses with each other. When the time comes to use your reply, this can help you (and the person asking) feel more comfortable.

Q. Are there specific resources for those suffering from secondary infertility?

A. Not as many as there ought to be, especially from a Christian perspective.

Perhaps the most thorough book on secondary infertility is *Wanting Another Child: Coping With Secondary Infertility* by Harriet Fishman Simons (Lexington Books, 1995). While not distinctly Christian in its approach, this book provides an excellent discussion of the emotional costs of secondary infertility on parents and the child(ren) they already have. Helpful personal stories and coping strategies are offered as well.

The Ache for a Child by Debra Bridwell (Micra Communications, 1999) contains an excellent chapter on secondary infertility from a Christian viewpoint.

Q. Can we find contentment with just one child?

A. The last thing we want is to be part of the "cheering section" which glibly tells you, "Be thankful for what you have," "Count your blessings," and "Just forget about wanting more." On the other hand, it's easy for all of us, fertile and infertile, to lose our perspective in the midst of pain.

Here are three things to remember:

1. *The "bedrock" truths.* In the heaving ocean of uncertainty, doubt, and baffling questions in which you find yourself, keep your eye on the promises of God. He promises that He knows and cares what's happening in our lives (Luke 12:6-7). He promises that sooner or later He works all things for our good and His glory (Romans 8:28). He promises that He will be with us to the end (Matthew 28:20). He promises that we can trust Him (Proverbs 3:5-6).

2. *That Satan is a thief.* He delights in stealing our joy whenever he can, and he's a master at it. He wants to prevent you from truly enjoying the child you have by leading you to obsess on what you don't have.

When you and your spouse bicker or worry incessantly about having another boy or girl, or when you're overwhelmed with sadness at your child's birthday, graduation, or other milestone because you fear you'll never enjoy these events with another child, the enemy has won a victory.

3. *That real contentment can't be found in having another child—or even a first one.* As someone once remarked: "True contentment can only be found in Christ—nothing more, nothing less, and nothing else!"

Susan, a friend, says it so well:

> Will I ever be satisfied with having only one child? Sometimes I think I am fine with just one child, and then something will trigger the old feelings again, like hearing from a friend who complains that she is "pregnant again."
>
> It helps me to remember that infertility is a journey, not a hundred-yard dash. It also helps to know that my Father sees how this journey will end. I may see only the next step in front of me, but He knows and controls my future. . . .
>
> Will there be another child for me/us? Will it be through birth or adoption? Can I learn to be content with one? Right now, I don't know the answers. I do know that God loves me and He will be there for me to the end. I will trust Him.

13

When Is It Time to Move On?

by John and Sylvia

We hope you're among the growing number of infertile couples who will eventually conceive and give birth to the child you want so much. But the truth is that even after extensive medical treatment, including the most advanced techniques, there are no guarantees.

Those who wrote the following understand this painful reality all too well:

> . . . The past two years have brought two miscarriages, eight rounds of Clomid, five rounds of *in vitro* fertilization (IVF) and many tears. The result? Our arms are still empty.

> . . . Our daughter, whom we named Heather, was due last January. She died *in utero* at 17 weeks. But this past January, I found out I was pregnant, and I just knew that finding out about this pregnancy a day after the due date for Heather was a blessing. I know that

God does not close a door unless He then opens a window. I carried this baby for 16 days, and then lost the baby to miscarriage. I know God has a plan for me.

. . . Our daughter and her husband just learned that their third IVF attempt has failed. Since each IVF procedure costs over $10,000, there is little money for another try. Even if the money was available, I am not sure that my daughter could stand the emotional turmoil of another failure. Is there anything I can do to encourage my daughter?

For these sufferers, and countless others like them, one question has to be faced sooner or later: "When should we stop medical treatment?"

Or to put it another way, when is enough enough?

THE HOUR OF DECISION

Perhaps you face that question now. When should you halt testing and treatment? When should you begin to redirect your focus from a determined pursuit of biological parenting to other goals?

It goes without saying that this is an extremely important and difficult decision. It's also one some of us *must* make if we're not to devote our whole lives to trying to get pregnant.

It's also a very personal decision. No one can give you a formula for making it. Each couple's decision will be based on factors whose importance only that couple can determine.

For some, this question answers itself. Friends of ours who were receiving treatment for infertility experienced two tubal pregnancies in two years. At first the possibility of reconstructive surgery for one of the tubes was raised; but the doctor, after studying the situation carefully, was forced to conclude that it was a forlorn hope.

Since this husband and wife have moral objections to assisted reproductive technology, they've reached the end of the medical road. They're now considering adoption.

For most couples, the matter never becomes that clear. They may continue treatment for years, unsure whether it will eventually result in pregnancy and childbirth.

Some couples find the decision to stop trying is triggered by change: a move to another city, a new career, being accepted by an adoption agency, or celebration of a milestone birthday. Others experience a slowly dawning awareness that enough time, energy, and money have been invested in the long marathon to have biological children—and it's time to redirect personal and financial resources.

How to Decide

If you find yourself in the uncomfortable position of trying to determine when enough is enough, consider the following.

1. *Face the facts.* If you've given the achievement of a pregnancy your "best shot," don't hesitate to ask your doctor to sit down with you and candidly discuss your prognosis.

If you do initiate such a conversation with your physician—or if he or she does—make it clear that you want an honest answer. The doctor may be relieved to hear this; he or she may have been looking for an opportunity to let you know where things really stand, but has been reluctant to do so for fear of causing hurt and disappointment.

2. *Both husband and wife should decide.* This is extremely important. When the decision is not reached by mutual agreement, you're creating a breeding ground for resentment ("I wish you hadn't stopped seeing Dr. Jones") or guilt ("If only I'd listened to my husband and tried one more time").

3. *Don't make a hasty decision.* Infertility testing and treatment involve a long, intensive, expensive process that's bound to produce anxiety and frustration. Understanding this and preparing yourselves for it can help you avoid the "early dropout syndrome." If you quit before you've really made an honest and thorough attempt to achieve a successful pregnancy, the two of you may regret it for the rest of your lives.

4. *Be willing to change your mind.* You may reach a point where you've had it. You're tired of monthly doctor visits, huge medical fees, and programmed sex. You're discouraged because there's no pregnancy after prolonged treatment, or you simply can't face another operation. You choose to terminate treatment.

Fine! But don't be afraid to change your mind. In six months or a year you may be refreshed and hopeful enough to try again. If so, don't be ashamed to call your doctor. You're not the first patients who changed their minds, nor will you be the last.

5. *Don't be unduly influenced by others.* Those around you—family members, close friends—may not understand why you're giving up. "How can you quit now?" they ask. "Why don't you give it more time?"

As a couple, you must decide when enough is enough. You know your situation and experience. Don't let outside pressure force you into "keeping on" when you've had enough.

6. *Take it to the Lord.* Make your decision a matter of sincere prayer as you seek God's guidance and wisdom. Be open to His direction. You may want to consult your pastor or mature Christian friends.

Once you've asked God for wisdom, assume He's given it to you: "If any of you lacks wisdom, he should ask God, who gives generously to all without finding fault, and it will be given to him. But when he asks, he must believe and not doubt, because he who doubts is like a wave of the sea, blown and tossed by the wind. That man should not think he will receive anything from the Lord; he is a double-minded man, unstable in all he does" (James 1:5-8).

The Next Step

Once you've determined that it's time to stop infertility treatment, what's next? Is this the end of the journey?

Not necessarily. There are more choices to make: Should you consider adoption? Foster parenting? Living positively without children?

We'll have more to say about the first of these options in the next chapter.

14

Are You Ready to Adopt?

by John and Sylvia

Not flesh of my flesh,
Nor bone of my bone,
But still miraculously
My own.
Never forget
For a single minute,
You didn't grow under my heart,
But in it.[1]

This poem, on the wall of Bethany Christian Services, greeted us during our first adoption interview. For us it became a living reality, for we were to become the parents of two beautiful, adopted children.

When infertile couples decide that enough is enough in terms of medical treatment, they often begin to explore alternatives. For many, adoption is number one on the list.

What Does God Say About Adoption?

Even though the Bible uses the word *adopt* only about four times, it refers to the *concept* of adoption surprisingly often. And when it does, the Bible always presents adoption as a positive, gracious act.

Moses, for example, was adopted by Pharaoh's daughter. His adoption, though sad for his Israelite parents, was part of God's plan for the deliverance of Israel from Egypt. Esther was "the girl Mordecai had adopted" (Esther 2:15). Her adoption also led to deliverance for God's people.

In a sense, Jesus was an adoptee too. Conceived by the Holy Spirit, Jesus was raised by Joseph, who was not His biological father. We think adopting parents can learn a great deal from Joseph, who unselfishly rearranged his life in order to provide Jesus with love, encouragement, and guidance.

The greatest adoption story in the Bible is God's adoption of believers. As the apostle Paul exults:

> Long before he laid down earth's foundations, [God] had us in mind, had settled on us as the focus of his love, to be made whole and holy by his love. Long, long ago he decided to adopt us into his family through Jesus Christ.
>
> Ephesians 1:4-5, *The Message*

God chose us because He wanted to. What a model this presents for those who want to adopt a child! For Christians struggling with infertility, adoption is not "second best." It's a way God can use for us to become loving parents.

Are You Prepared?

Before you get too enthused about adoption, make sure you understand not only the process, but yourself. Here are six ways to do that.

1. *Be sure you really want and will accept an adopted child.* Adoption isn't for everyone. No one should go on a guilt trip because he or she isn't ready to accept an adopted child.

A friend who recently experienced a miscarriage after infertility told us that, for her, adoption was out. "Being pregnant was such a special feeling," she said. "I just couldn't go any other way to have a baby." She may change her mind—but for now adoption is not for her, and that is legitimate.

A variety of reasons lead some couples to believe that adoption is not for them. That's okay. Couples who experience long-term infertility sometimes get tremendous pressure from family, friends, or even church leaders to "just adopt." We're convinced that adoption is a calling from God; some are called to become adoptive parents, and others aren't.

2. *Be aware of unresolved issues.* Some adoption workers and agencies believe that all issues of infertility, including grief and loss, must be totally resolved before a couple is ready to adopt. We disagree; many couples continue to deal with infertility issues even after adopting successfully.

On the other hand, the following questions ought to be asked—and answered—by couples before they consider themselves emotionally and psychologically ready to adopt:

• Have you begun losing energy for more infertility treatments, and do you dread your next doctor's appointment?

• Is having a child to love more important to you than how the child joins your family?

• Have you grieved the loss of your dream child?

• Have you gained some honest and realistic knowledge about adoption?[2]

3. *Be honest about your motives.* Can you look over the following list of *wrong* reasons to adopt and conclude that they are *not* yours?

"We will be doing the poor child a favor."

"Our other children will have a playmate."

"We've been through a difficult infertility experience and we deserve a baby."

"Raising a baby will help our marriage."

"Having a baby to love will make me feel completed."

4. *Be prepared for imperfect children.* Adoptive couples often have an idealized concept of the baby that awaits them. Adoption workers sometimes call this the "baby-doll syndrome."

If you're looking for a perfect baby, it's time for a reality check. There are none—adopted or biological. Like all children, adopted ones come with a history; sometimes it's fairly uneventful, but sometimes it's not altogether pretty.

Adoption workers are obligated to provide you with full disclosure regarding a birth parent's medical history, if there is any chance that history will affect your child's health. If, for example, the birth mother is a known alcohol or drug user, the adoption agency will disclose that information. Sometimes the medical history is sketchy because the birth father is unavailable to interview, or the birth mother is not totally forthcoming.

In any event, there are no perfect babies. There are only imperfect ones who need the love and care of families who are willing to open their hearts and homes.

5. *Be prepared for the expense.* When it comes to adoption costs, there's bad news and good news. The bad news is that couples who adopt a healthy infant through a reputable agency can expect to pay from $8,000 to $20,000. Adopting internationally can be even more expensive, depending on the child's country of origin. Some nations, such as Russia, may require one or two trips to the country before you can adopt a child. Other countries, such as Korea, do not have such a requirement.

Then there's the good news. Some agencies, including Bethany Christian Services, have a sliding fee scale for lower income families. Also, some agencies and many state adoption programs have older or special needs children who can be adopted at little or no cost. It takes a special calling to parent such a youngster, but it can be a wonderful opportunity to express Christ's love to a child who needs a home.

Perhaps the best news is that, if you're a U.S. citizen, you're probably eligible for the Adoption Expense Tax Credit. This represents significant savings in the cost of adoption. At this writing the tax credit for adoption expenses is up to $10,000. Those who adopt a special needs child are eligible for a $10,000 credit even if they incur no adoption expenses. For more details check with your tax consultant, or search the Internet for "Adoption Expense Credit."

6. *Be prepared for joy!* The foregoing cautions may have you wondering, "Are the authors really in favor of adoption?" The answer is an enthusiastic yes. For us, adoption has been a very positive experience. We wouldn't trade for anything the opportunity we've had to enjoy and raise our two adopted children.

Having experienced the birth of a biological child after adopting two, we've known both ways of becoming parents. Yes, becoming pregnant and enjoying the thrill of childbirth is wonderful and unique. But there's no less joy, wonderment, or thrill in receiving a phone call from an adoption agency or networking contact saying, "We may have a baby for you!" Suddenly your life, which may have seemed stagnant and colorless, is brightly painted with hopes, opportunities, and possibilities.

In many cases the joy is shared. Adoptive parents are often overwhelmed with support; friends and relatives frequently get almost as excited as the adopting parents. Adopting couples tend to receive more baby cards, gifts, and words of congratulations than those who have a biological child.

On the Sunday when we announced in church that we'd adopted a baby, one elderly man started clapping wildly. Later we received gifts from people we hardly knew. For us, as for many adoptive parents, the celebration became a communal experience.

READY? SET? GO!

When you're ready to seriously explore adoption, here are some of the steps you'll need to take.

1. *Contact a local agency.* We admit it—we're biased toward agency adoptions. It's true that thousands of satisfied parents have gone to attorneys to facilitate adoption; that's fine. We prefer agencies because we believe they're less expensive, and that they provide more pre- and post-placement counseling than an attorney can. It's also more likely that an agency will have a skilled adoption worker present at a hospital placement, a time when emotions are running high.

At the end of this chapter we list resources to help you find a good agency. Personally, we deeply appreciate Christian agencies for whom adoption is not just a business, but a ministry.

2. *Attend informational meetings.* Agencies hold public information meetings throughout the year for prospective adoptive parents. There you'll probably meet adoptive parents and birthparents who've made an adoption plan. You'll also learn about the application process, fees, requirements, and types of adoption offered.

Now's the time to think about the type of adoption you want to pursue. Are you committed to a confidential (closed) adoption, or would you consider something more open (more on this later in the chapter)? Do you want to adopt a baby, an older child, a child of another race, a child with special needs? Are you thinking only of domestic adoption, or considering international as well?

Our advice is to be open to the leading of the Holy Spirit. You never know what the Lord might have in mind when it comes to adoption.

Here's just one example.

Several years ago, in a small Romanian village, a baby boy was born. Instead of bringing joy to his parents, his birth brought despair. His family loved him dearly, but other villagers turned away in disgust. Little

George had been born without arms, and the villagers viewed his birth as a curse from God.

Raising George in that village became impossible. George's mother was determined to find a place where the boy could be loved unconditionally.

Through the International Adoption Program of Bethany Christian Services, Mike and Sharon Dennehy of Hebron, Connecticut, heard about George. They were determined that, arms or no arms, he would have a place in their hearts and home.

Nine years later, George is thriving with the Dennehys. He has energy to burn, a lot of friends, and is doing well in school. He's even developed a passion for playing the cello, and is a member of the Bach Academy Orchestra.

That's not all. Mike and Sharon decided to adopt a second son, James, who also has no arms. James, age seven, also plays cello for the Bach Academy Orchestra.

Wait—there's more! The conductor of the orchestra was so impressed by George and his brother that she and her husband decided to adopt a child of their own. And guess what? Their child, a daughter, has no arms either—and at three years old is already beginning to show interest in the cello. Who knows? Maybe someday these three kids will form their own trio![3]

3. *Complete an application and undergo an adoptive family assessment.* For most couples this is the least attractive part of the process. As one person put it: "Those who have biological children do not have to prove their worthiness to be parents, but we do! It doesn't seem fair."

Perhaps not—but agencies are responsible for the welfare of those in their care. They want to make sure children are placed in good homes.

Filling out an application and undergoing a home study may not be fun, but it's not nearly as distasteful as many assume. This is especially true of the home study. Many infertile couples, desperate to adopt a baby, turn themselves into Nervous Nellies at the thought of a social worker coming to inspect their home.

Matt and Sally, for instance, are getting ready for their home study. Not much of a housekeeper by nature, Sally has fretted all week about Thursday afternoon when the agency worker is expected. On Monday she has new carpet put down in the living room. On Tuesday she cleans the bedrooms and basement. On Wednesday she dusts in places she hasn't dusted in 10 years. That night she sleeps nary a wink.

Finally, on Thursday afternoon, nervous and tired, she and her husband welcome the social worker. Everything seems to be going well until their visitor casually asks, "How many bedrooms do you have?"

Sally panics. "Right now we only have two," she blurts out. "Do we need another bedroom? We'll gladly build one if you require it!"

Nervousness in the face of a home study is unnecessary. Your home doesn't have to be "white glove" clean, the social worker won't look under your bed, and you won't need an extra bedroom. The home study is simply an opportunity for the agency to know you better in your own surroundings, and to determine that your home meets minimum requirements to provide a good environment for a child.

4. *Prepare an adoptive family profile.* For infant adoptions, this is a very important part of the process. Today, agencies do not typically choose families for babies; birth moms select an adoptive family from family profiles.

Your profile would contain a brief description of you and your spouse and why you would make wonderful parents, usually along with pictures of yourselves and your home. You're "marketing" yourselves to prospective birth moms, so care must be taken to present yourselves in the best light.

Handsome, young, and wealthy couples tend to be chosen before older, plain, and heavier ones—even though the latter might make wonderful parents. Thankfully, some birth parents' preferences aren't just skin deep. As one birth mother put it, "My parents were older when I was born, and I felt they always had time for me—I want my baby in that kind of home."

Many agencies post adoptive family profiles on their Web sites for birth parents to peruse. For samples, check the Bethany site at www.bethany.org.

5. *Pray, wait, and network.* After you've been placed on the waiting family list, it's time to be patient, prayerful—and proactive. Some birth parents and adoptive families find each other through networking—making personal connections. Some would-be adoptive parents send fliers to every obstetrician/gynecologist in the community, place ads in local newspapers, talk to colleagues at work, or write letters to relatives across the country, informing them of a desire to adopt.

One never knows how the Lord may work. While talking with his boss one day, a man named Jim mentioned that he and his wife were trying to adopt. His boss was surprised. "I didn't know you and Karen were interested in adopting," he said. "Our neighbors have a daughter who is unmarried and pregnant. I know that she is thinking about adoption."

Some adoption agencies encourage families to network and may offer a discounted fee to those who find a baby in this way. Check with your agency to find out about its policies.

IS OPENNESS OKAY?[4]

When we talk to infertile couples about open adoptions, we're often met with cold looks of fear and resistance. The majority of prospective adoptive families are, at least initially, opposed to the concept of openness.

An open adoption maintains some level of continuing contact between the birthparent(s), the adopted child, and the adoptive family. The type and frequency of contact vary widely, ranging from the occasional exchange of pictures through an agency to regular, face-to-face meetings.

It's not unusual for open adoptions to reach such high levels of trust that adoptive parents think of the birth mother as a younger sister. Some adoptive parents even leave their child with the birth mom occasionally while they go on a weekend getaway.

We fully understand the apprehension many couples feel about openness. When we adopted our son years ago, openness was not an option. Neither we nor our son had any contact with his birth parents.

At the time, we wouldn't have had it any other way. As far as we were concerned, his birth parents had released him, and he belonged solely to us. Our commitment to a closed adoption was fed by our nagging fear that the birth parents might change their minds and want him back. Our son was such a cute little guy, with black, curly hair and round cheeks, that we were haunted by the notion that one of his birth parents might find him and steal him away.

Today, however, our feelings about openness have moved 180 degrees. The more we've listened to adoption experts, adoptive parents, and adoptees themselves, the more we've come to value openness.

Why? Because we now realize that the pros considerably outweigh the cons in this type of adoption. Most open adoptions offer significant benefits to each member of the adoption triad—adopted child, birth parents, and adoptive parents. Consider the following.

Openness benefits the adopted child. Is it better for an adopted child to have some knowledge of and contact with his or her birthparents, or for them to remain anonymous and hidden? The former is significantly better than the latter.

One of the most important tasks of childhood is to answer the question "Who am I?" When our son was in fifth grade, one of his assignments at school was to write a report on his ethnic heritage. He came home and said, "I know you guys are Dutch (with a name like Van Regenmorter, how did he know?). But what am I? Am I Dutch, too?" He was in the process of discovering who he was.

Dr. Ron Nydam, in his book *Adoptees Come of Age,* speaks of this in terms of a puzzle. In trying to answer the "Who am I?" question, many adoptees feel they're missing pieces. Nydam recounts the story of a 22-year-old woman named Wendy whose only knowledge of her birth mother came after the birth mother had died. Wendy determined that she would at least visit the grave, even though it required traveling out of state. When she arrived, she saw an etching of her birth mother's face on the gravestone. She exclaimed that she had seen herself in the outline. Even that was an important discovery of something about herself.[5]

Kristine Faasse, an adoption supervisor at Bethany Christian Services, says it this way:

> All children want to know their story. They want to know who they look like, act like, and where they come from. If children do not know the answers to these questions, they invent the answers. They invent what are known as "ghost parents." That is, in the absence of factual information about birth parents, adopted children often fantasize about Birthmom and Birthdad, and what life would be like with them. Sometimes adopted children create parents who are movie stars or millionaires. At other times adoptees create birthparents in a darker light—"Why were they so uncaring, selfish, and thoughtless that they were unwilling to do what it takes to make a family?"

Is it healthier for an adoptee to know his or her birth parents, or to imagine what they're like? What if there is indeed a dark side to the birth parents' lives? Wouldn't it be better to shield adoptees from the truth?

Nydam answers those questions bluntly: "Even bad news about birthparents is good news for an adoptee, because it is *real* news."[6]

Openness benefits birth parents. Birth parents make an agonizing decision when they release their child for adoption. Often they wonder, "Did I do the right thing?" "Is my baby okay?" "Does he/she have a good home?"

In an open adoption birth parents don't have to wonder and fear. They have the opportunity to know that their child is in a loving, caring, Christian home.

Openness benefits adoptive parents. How? By giving them more knowledge of their child's history. Knowing one or both birth parents can help adoptive parents better understand the child. In an open adoption, adoptive parents might be able to say, "Ah, now I know why she likes colorful clothes," or "Maybe that's why he has such an aptitude for working on machines."

Above all, openness benefits adoptive parents because the worry is gone. No longer are they likely to feel that cold, unreasoning fear that a birth parent wants the baby back. Kristine Faasse's experience leads her to believe that adoptive parents who meet birth parents feel entitled to raise their child—free from anxiety.

Still, openness may not be for everyone. For this reason many agencies, including Bethany Christian Services, also offer confidential (closed) adoptions. Adoptive families should choose an arrangement that's best for their circumstances. If we had the choice today between an open adoption and one that's closed, though, there's no doubt which road we would travel.

ADOPTION RESOURCES

Here are organizations, publications, and Web sites to help you if you're exploring the option of adoption.

Adoption Guide
Hope Communications LLC
42 West 38th St., Suite 901
New York, NY 10018
www.adoptivefamilies.com

This annual guide from the publisher of *Adoptive Families Magazine* offers practical information, including a state-by-state listing of adoption agencies and state adoption units.

Bethany Christian Services
901 Eastern Ave. NE
P.O. Box 294
Grand Rapids, MI 49501-0294
www.bethany.org
1-800-BETHANY
Bethany is a pro-life, Christian adoption and family services agency with 75 offices in the United States and 13 international offices.

Child Welfare League of America, Inc. (CWLA)
440 First Street NW, Thrid Floor
Washington, DC 20001-2085
www.cwla.org
(202) 638-2952
The CWLA publishes information on adoption including an adoption directory.

Holt International Children's Services
P.O. Box 2880
Eugene, OR 97402
www.holtintl.org
(541) 687-2202
Holt is a Christian adoption agency specializing in adoptions from Korea.

National Adoption Information Clearinghouse (NAIC)
330 C St. SW
Washington, DC 20447

www.calib.com/naic

(888) 251-0075

The NAIC offers valuable information on adoption resources, including ideas on how to make adoption affordable.

The North American Council on Adoptable Children

970 Raymond Ave., Suite 106

Saint Paul, MN 55114-1149

www.nacac.org

(651) 644-3036

This national organization provides information on and advocacy for adopting children who have special needs.

Additional Web-based information:

www.adoption.com

www.adoption.about.com

www.adopting.org

This is only a partial list. Try a search on the Web for other resources and services in your area. In addition to public agencies, a variety of Christian adoption organizations may be available in your region.

15

When Will the
Journey End?

by Sylvia

After 8 years of infertility I am still hurting, still heavy-hearted and
unable to deal with surrounding pregnancies. My arms are still empty.

—Jill

I don't know where my infertility road will end, but I am about
ready to give up. I am exhausted physically, financially, and spiritually. I am wondering if I should close this chapter in my life.

—Rhonda

More than 40 years ago Granger Westberg wrote a classic book, still
used by grief counselors today. Its title: *Good Grief.*[1]

Westberg argues convincingly that whenever we experience a significant loss—the death of a loved one, the end of a relationship, a painful
career termination—our grief will follow a predictable path.

The journey of infertility—particularly if it's long, with no end in sight—is a grief experience. It tends to follow a certain path, or series of milestones. In the first chapter of this book I described several of those milestones:

Shock ("I'm sorry, Mrs. Jones, but you have stage-four endometriosis.")

Denial ("There must be some mistake!")

Anger ("Why can't you go with me to the next doctor's appointment?")

Guilt ("Why is God punishing me?")

Depression ("Why do I feel so dragged out and unattractive?")

Isolation ("I don't know where I fit in anymore!")

In this concluding chapter I'll describe the final stages of the journey of infertility. You may recognize yourself at mileposts along the way. If so, you'll know how far you've come—and how far you have yet to travel before reaching the God-given acceptance every infertile couple needs.

Please remember that the stages of grief as described by Westberg end with *recovery*, not *despair*. The road before you is not endless! I can't promise that your journey will end quickly, or even in the manner you presently desire, but it will end.

Right now you may be full of anxiety, doubt, and discouragement. But when God is in the mix of our lives, amazing and unanticipated recovery can happen. For some of us, He may sneak up gradually, unobserved, moving us quietly and slowly toward resolution and peace. For others, His work is more obvious and sudden as He surprises us with unexpected joy.

With that in mind, come with me on the final miles of the journey of infertility.

AMBIVALENCE

Before the journey ends, it's very possible that you'll climb the uncertain slopes of ambivalence.

When you're ambivalent, you aren't sure how you feel. At one moment your longing to have children reaches the point of desperation. At the next you tell yourself you don't care if you ever have them. When your friend comes over with her baby, you alternate between wanting to grab that infant out of her arms and wanting to push him or her away and out of sight.

An Oasis of Calm

This is a little rest period in your journey. You may experience it when you decide to give your body a break from all the medications you've been taking. Or you may find it when you decide to quit active treatment for a while and just live a normal life with your spouse. Or perhaps you'll spend time there as you finally, after much restless soul-searching and prayer, reach a decision about whether to try one last IVF-ET attempt.

In any case, it's a much-needed respite from the journey. You may feel a sense of sadness that you haven't achieved your goal, but it's a calm sadness. This oasis of calm can be a time to prepare for the emotional work to come.

The River of Grief

The most difficult part of the journey is through the river of grief.

You may reach it as a result of a doctor's report: "I'm so sorry, Pam, but I have bad news; this IVF has failed too. I really can't recommend another attempt."

Or you may be plunged into this stream by another sudden pregnancy loss—and this time you and your spouse agree that you'll stop trying to become pregnant.

Or perhaps you begin this part of your journey because the ticking of your biological clock has grown ever louder. You experience the gnawing realization that you'll probably never be a biological parent.

In many respects your grief will be what counselors term *disenfranchised grief.* That is, your sense of loss will not be openly acknowledged, socially sanctioned, or publicly mourned. For unless your grief results from a late-term pregnancy loss or infant death, there will be no body, no casket, no memorial service held in church. Chances are that no friends will offer you condolences. It is the death of a dream; it is the death of your hopes and aspirations. It is the death of a child you never had.

During this time of grief, all the emotions you felt before—anger, denial, guilt, depression, you name it—may resurface with a vengeance. Perhaps you can't concentrate on your work. You may have difficulty sleeping. The loss becomes more and more real, first in spurts and flashes, and then in a long, unremitting stream.

You may not realize it at the time, but during this stage of your journey you will accomplish a great deal of emotional work—work necessary for you to reach the end of the journey. This involves the process of burying those dreams that have died.

What have you lost due to infertility, miscarriage, or infant death? A son who looks like his dad? A daughter who looks like her mom? You begin to bury the dreams and you mourn.

Were you hoping that someday you could pass on your mother's crystal chandelier to your daughter? To announce to Grandma that you were finally expecting? To experience pregnancy, childbirth, breastfeeding? You bury these dreams and you mourn.

It's difficult to bury your dreams and hopes. Some you may not bury completely. But at least you begin the process.

A CHANGE OF DIRECTION

Having grieved and mourned, you begin the journey again. You're through the most difficult part. You're on your way to recovery.

It begins when you take one small step toward a positive goal and feel a budding interest in the future. You marshal the energy that used to go into grief and start devoting it to new projects and new beginnings.

The room you may have been keeping for the baby might be transformed into a study. You start to cultivate whatever is fertile in your life—a hobby you've neglected, a career you've put on hold, or more education in a field that interests you.

Maybe you decide to write a book or travel or do short-term missionary work. Or perhaps you dedicate yourself to being an awesome "uncle and aunt" to kids in your neighborhood who are semi-neglected and starving for adult attention.

You begin to see that the possibilities for taking positive steps are endless. This is the stage for new plans, new dreams.

RECOVERY

When you begin to make those plans and dream those dreams, when you discover new projects that deserve your energy and time, you are well on the road to recovery.

That doesn't mean there won't be sudden, painful moments or that the tears will never fall. They will.

> She sat on the bus,
> Intently reading a book
> Filled with another's experience.
> Hoping to find an answer within its pages.
> The bus lurched forward
> Causing her to look up.
> They were directly across from her
> More pain in plain view.
> One of young age, not yet twenty,
> A bottle of milk thrust into her jacket pocket.

Another of older age, tattooed, in need of a haircut.
The one with them, clothed in pink polka dots.
As she resumed reading, she could barely contain
The rage that had resurfaced,
An old rage that screamed of infertile unfairness.
Thankfully, she heard another voice as well.
A still, small whisper which said:
"My thoughts are not your thoughts,
neither are your ways my ways," declares the LORD.
"As the heavens are higher than the earth,
so are my ways higher than your ways
and my thoughts than your thoughts" (Isaiah 55:8-9).[2]

Recovery does not mean that all the pain is gone. It means that your infertility is no longer the dominant, consuming force it once was—and that other life-affirming goals have taken its place.

SURPRISE!

Be warned: At any point on the journey, even after you've mourned and moved on, surprises can happen.

I am living proof. Fourteen years after we married, long after we'd adopted and discontinued infertility treatment, the Lord surprised us with a successful pregnancy.

Others have experienced different surprises, long after all hope of parenting has died and goals have changed. Todd and Carol, for example, battled infertility for 10 years—including several failed IVF-ET attempts—before they called it quits. They built a new house, began raising horses, and were planning on remaining a family of two.

Todd declared they would never adopt. "I don't think I could ever love an adopted child in the same way I would love 'my own,'" he insisted.

A few months later an elderly woman from their neighborhood approached them. They knew her only casually, but she said: "Maybe you have noticed the little boy and girl who have been living with us. We are their grandparents. Since my daughter has been in and out of trouble with the law and is not able to care for them anymore, she has relinquished full custody to us."

Then, with tears in her eyes, the woman made a startling request: "We are too old to raise children; would you be interested in adopting them?"

Hesitant at first, Todd and Carol agreed to meet the children. Within 20 minutes Todd was on the floor playing trucks with the little boy, and Carol had the little girl on her lap. That was it! Today, Todd and Carol are proud adoptive parents.

Even when the unexpected doesn't happen, the journey need not end in unhappiness. As Tammy Anderson observes:

> So many times we think that the only "happy ending" to an infertile couple's struggle comes when God blesses them with a child. But what about the couple for whom God has a different plan—a plan in which the couple remains a family of two? Is this couple any "less blessed" or unfulfilled? . . . God showed me how I can be available to others in ways that I would not be available if I had kids, perhaps as an aunt or a cherished friend. God has shown me what a blessing my life is, and that my husband and I can have a "happy ending" to our infertility, with or without child.[3]

If your journey ends without the arrival of children, biologically or through adoption, please remember that there is no reason to feel guilty about remaining child-free. As one woman discovered, "My husband and I prayed and waited months, which turned into years, for direction. The answer always seemed to be the same for both of us . . . acceptance."

Contrary to popular opinion, God has never indicated that children are necessary for happiness in marriage. As one preacher has noted: "In the second chapter of Genesis God declares, 'A man will leave his father and mother and be united to his wife and they will become one flesh' and there is a period there" (v. 24). A Christian husband and wife can find fulfillment in each other and in service to the Lord, with or without children.

Couples without children can pursue avenues of Christian service which would be difficult for couples with children. Mentoring disadvantaged or special needs youngsters is a possibility; so is becoming "sons and daughters" to older persons who have no children to care for them. One childless husband and wife we know open their home to children who attend the local school for the deaf. Another couple serves in a ministry that takes groups of young people on service project trips.

Still others have become licensed foster care families through local adoption agencies. One foster mom has called it "a road less traveled," but a rewarding one. As she describes it:

> We are now the foster parents to a special nine-year-old boy. We never thought fostering would be as fulfilling as it has turned out to be. Sure, there are rough times, but the good definitely outweighs the bad. . . . It's as if he is ours—"on loan" from the Lord—to comfort and mend the damage that has been done to him in the past. When our job is finished, our door is always open for another child in need of our love, support, and direction.[4]

ACCEPTANCE AND PEACE

Finally, in the uniqueness of God's loving plan for you, you reach the end of the journey. You are home.

You've reached a God-given sense of peace and acceptance. Your faith has returned in full force. For a long time you asked, "Why me, God?" but now that question has lost its sharp edges.

In His infinite wisdom, God has not miraculously lifted the burden of infertility from your shoulders. He has been there all along, helping you carry it, and that is enough. Once again you can read Psalm 106:1 with a smile on your face instead of through tears: "Praise the LORD. Give thanks to the LORD, for he is good; his love endures forever."

You feel more optimistic. Life regains its full flavor, rich with opportunities for enjoyment and service.

You can share your loss without bitterness. You find it less difficult to love your best friend's baby. You sense the needs of others and begin to see that God is using your infertility to make you more compassionate about their loss and hurts.

DOES EVERY INFERTILE PERSON TRAVEL THIS JOURNEY?

Probably every infertile person travels at least a portion of the road. But not everyone makes the journey in exactly the sequence outlined here.

For some, the journey is not as intense; for others it is more intense. Some go through all the stages; others don't. Some move forward, then find themselves slipping backward temporarily.

Some couples get "stuck" along the way. Rather than moving to the next stage, they become mired deep in an emotional impasse.

Some may stop at the point of depression. Instead of experiencing the mild depression that almost every infertile person feels at one time or other, they find themselves severely depressed and unable to function. Others may become stuck at the point of isolation, so much so that a wedge between husband and wife develops and divorce is considered.

If you become stuck along the journey, take action. Let a professional counselor help you move closer to your destination of recovery.

THE "OLD FRIEND"

Once you've spent significant time on the journey of infertility, you'll never be able to forget it completely. There will always be moments when it brings a stab of pain.

Barbara Eck Menning, founder of RESOLVE, calls infertility "an old friend" that will always be part of her life:

> My infertility resides in my heart as an old friend. I do not hear
> from it for weeks at a time, and then, a moment, a thought, a baby
> announcement or some such thing, and I will feel the tug—maybe
> even be sad or shed a few tears. And I think, "There's my old friend.
> It will always be a part of me . . ."[5]

Many of us know that "old friend."

Thankfully, those of us who know the Lord Jesus have an infinitely better and stronger Friend who will always be part of our lives.

This Friend will never leave us or forsake us (Hebrews 13:5).

This Friend will transform our sorrows (Romans 8:28).

This Friend will stay closer to us than a sister or brother (Proverbs 18:24).

With this Friend, even when the road is long and the mountains are high, we can say: "I can do everything through him who gives me strength" (Philippians 4:13).

Notes

∞

THERE IS AN EMPTY ROOM
1. Adapted from Garcia, Stephanie, "There is an Empty Room," *Stepping Stones Newsletter* (June/July 2002), p. 4.

CHAPTER 2: PITFALLS ALONG THE PATH
1. McIlhaney, Joe S., Jr., M.D. with Nethery, Susan, *1001 Health-Care Questions Women Ask* (Grand Rapids, Mich.: Baker Books, 1998), p. 434.
2. Keenan, Jeffrey A., M.D., "Infertility: Facts and Fiction," *Stepping Stones Newsletter* (October/November 2000), p. 2.
3. From comments made at a conference for infertile couples sponsored by Stepping Stones at Bethany Christian Services, May 4, 2000.

CHAPTER 3: WHY DOES INFERTILITY HURT SO MUCH?
1. Schalesky, Marlo, *Empty Womb, Aching Heart* (Minneapolis: Bethany House, 2001), pp. 15-16.

CHAPTER 4: HOW CAN YOU COPE WHILE YOU HOPE?
1. From an illustration shared at a ministry conference sponsored by the Willow Creek Association, at Willow Creek Community Church, South Barrington, Illinois, 1996.
2. Sometimes we wonder how many couples whom "God has joined together" have been "torn asunder" by the harsh realities

of long-term infertility. The only research we've found on this subject was a Ph.D. study by Frank van Balen, who found an increased rate of divorce by almost a factor of two among childless couples. More study on this question is necessary.

3. Christenson, Evelyn, *What Happens When Women Pray* (Colorado Springs, Colo.: ChariotVictor, 1991), pp. 23-24. © 1975, 1991 by Cook Communications Ministries. Copied with permission. May not be further reproduced. All rights reserved.

CHAPTER 5: HANDLING THE HOLIDAYS

1. Dobson, James, "A Holiday Message by Dr. James Dobson," *Family News from Dr. James Dobson*, a newsletter published by Focus on the Family (December 1998), p. 1.
2. *RESOLVE Newsletter* (December 1989).

CHAPTER 6: HOW TO KEEP YOUR MARRIAGE STRONG

1. Van Balen, Frank, *A Life Without Children. Involuntary Childlessness: Experience, Stress and Adaptation* (Assen, Netherlands: Dekker and Van de Vegt, 1991).
2. Fabry, Chris, "Is Your Husband a H.I.M.?" *Focus on the Family* (February 1999), p. 3. This article is adapted from *The H.I.M. Book: A Woman's Manual for Understanding Her Highly Identifiable Male* (Colorado Springs, Colo.: Waterbrook Press, 1997). © 1997 by Christopher H. Fabry. Used by permission of Waterbrook Press. All rights reserved.
3. Bashford, Robert, M.D., "Psychological Aspects of Infertility," *CNS Spectrums: The International Journal of Neuropsychiatric Medicine* (April 1999), p. 67.
4. McIlhaney, Joe S., M.D., and Van Regenmorter, John and Sylvia, *Dear God, Why Can't We Have a Baby?* (Grand Rapids, Mich.: Baker Book House, 1986), pp. 71-72. In 2001, Ann McAllister,

Ph.D., L.C.S.W., completed a research study titled, "An Exploratory Study of Gender Differences in Parenting Styles Used and in Continuing Sense of Loss." She reports, "Scores earned by participants [experiencing infertility] were compared to scores earned by a group of persons who had experienced a death within the past year. Overall the men earned lower scores than women in the study. . . . Women had significantly higher scores than men in six clinical areas of grief, despair, anger/hostility, social isolation, loss of control, rumination, and depersonalization."

5. Ibid., p. 72.
6. Philip Nienhuis, M.S.W., is a family therapist at Bethany Christian Services, Grand Rapids, Michigan.
7. Botsios, Colleen, "Julia Child . . . less," RESOLVE newsletter of Dallas/Fort Worth, Texas (January/February 1990), as quoted by Glahn, Sandra and Cutrer, William, M.D., *When Empty Arms Become a Heavy Burden* (Nashville: Broadman and Holman, 1997), pp. 42-44.

CHAPTER 7: WHAT DO YOU SAY TO AUNT SALLY?

1. From "Infertility: Myths and Facts," "RESOLVE Fact Sheet" found at www.resolve.org.
2. We're grateful to Catherine Ward-Long, editor of *Anna's Journal*, for sending us this information. The dates and days have been changed to protect the church's identity.

CHAPTER 8: FAITH AND INFERTILITY: THE NAGGING QUESTION

1. Yancey, Philip, *Where Is God When It Hurts?* (Grand Rapids, Mich.: Zondervan, 1990), p. 84.
2. Ibid., p. 81.
3. Dobson, James, *When God Doesn't Make Sense* (Wheaton, Ill.: Tyndale House Publishers, 1993), pp. 17-18.

4. Excerpted from the poem "It's in the Valleys I Grow" by Jane Eggleston. Extensive research has failed to find a copyrighted source; the poem has been reproduced on a number of Internet sites.

5. Eareckson Tada, Joni and Estes, Steve, *A Step Further* (Grand Rapids, Mich.: Zondervan, 2001), pp. 170-71. © 1978, 1990, 2001 by Joni Eareckson Tada. Used by permission of Zondervan.

6. *The Heidelberg Catechism* (Grand Rapids, Mich.: CRC Publications, 1988 revised edition), p. 22.

CHAPTER 9: HOW SHALL WE THEN PRAY?

1. DeVries, Michael, *The Banner* (January 8, 1983), p. 23.

2. *The Heidelberg Catechism*, p. 68.

3. DeVries, *op. cit.*, p. 23.

CHAPTER 10: HIGH-TECH TREATMENTS: TOUGH ISSUES

1. Dobson, James, *Complete Marriage and Family Home Reference Guide* (Wheaton, Ill.: Tyndale House Publishers, 2000), pp. 389-90.

2. Glahn and Cutrer, *When Empty Arms Become a Heavy Burden*, p. 170.

3. Dobson, *Complete Marriage and Family Home Reference Guide*, pp. 389-91.

4. Koeman, Ken, *The Banner* (August 30, 1998), p. 28.

CHAPTER 11: PREGNANCY LOSS AND INFANT DEATH

1. Roskamp, Jackie, *Quest for a Silent God: Struggling with the Agony of Infertility and Multiple Infant Loss While Searching for God,* an unpublished manuscript.

2. Siebers, Kristin, "Dear Little One," *Stepping Stones Newsletter* (August/September 2002), p. 4.

3. Excerpted from Doughman, Johni, "Precious Angel Babies," unpublished.

4. Adapted from a presentation made at Bethany Christian Services (June 1998). Nancy S. Kingma is bereavement coordinator for Spectrum Health, Grand Rapids, Michigan.

CHAPTER 12: SECONDARY INFERTILITY: A MISUNDERSTOOD PAIN

1. Rubin, Rita, "Just One Child Can Leave an Empty Space," *USA Today* (October 13, 1998), p. 11D.

2. Bridwell, Debra, *The Ache for a Child* (Lafayette, Colo.: Micra Communications, 1999), p. 247.

3. Ibid., p. 249.

CHAPTER 14: ARE YOU READY TO ADOPT?

1. Heyliger, Fleur Conkling, "Not Flesh of My Flesh," *The Saturday Evening Post* (1952). Reprinted with permission of *The Saturday Evening Post*, © 1952 (renewed), BFL&MS, Inc., Indianapolis.

2. Adapted from Walker, Elaine, *Loving Journey's Guide to Adoption* (Peterborough, N.H.: Loving Journeys, 1992), p. 47.

3. Van Regenmorter, John, "But God . . ." *Lifelines*, published by Bethany Christian Services (summer 2003), p. 10.

4. Parts of this section are adapted from our article "Open Adoption—a Good Option?" *The Banner* (January 2003), pp. 22-23.

5. Nydam, Ronald, *Adoptees Come of Age* (Louisville, Ky.: Westminster Press, 1999), p. 48.

6. Ibid., p. 109.

CHAPTER 15: WHEN WILL THE JOURNEY END?

1. Minneapolis: Augsburg Press, 1962.
2. Bohdan, Sharon, "Infertility Unfairness," *Stepping Stones Newsletter* (August/September 2001), p. 6.
3. Anderson, Tammy, "Is There Only One Happy Ending?" *Stepping Stones Newsletter* (February/March 2002), p. 3.
4. Fasnacht, Janet, "A Road Less Traveled," *Stepping Stones Newsletter* (February/March 2001), pp. 1-2.
5. Menning, B. E., *Infertility: A Guide for the Childless Couple* (Englewood Cliffs, N.J.: Prentice Hall, 1977), p. 117.

FOCUS ON THE FAMILY®

Welcome to the Family!

Whether you received this book as a gift, borrowed it from a friend, or purchased it yourself, we're glad you read it! It's just one of the many helpful, insightful, and encouraging resources produced by Focus on the Family.

In fact, that's what Focus on the Family is all about—providing inspiration, information, and biblically based advice to people in all stages of life.

It began in 1977 with the vision of one man, Dr. James Dobson, a licensed psychologist and author of 16 best-selling books on marriage, parenting, and family. Alarmed by the societal, political, and economic pressures that were threatening the existence of the American family, Dr. Dobson founded Focus on the Family with one employee—an assistant—and a once-a-week radio broadcast, aired on only 36 stations.

Now an international organization, Focus on the Family is dedicated to preserving Judeo-Christian values and strengthening the family through more than 70 different ministries, including eight separate daily radio broadcasts; television public service announcements; 10 publications; and a steady series of books and award-winning films and videos for people of all ages and interests.

Recognizing the needs of, as well as the sacrifices and important contributions made by, such diverse groups as educators, physicians, attorneys, crisis pregnancy center staff, and single parents, Focus on the Family offers specific outreaches to uphold and minister to these individuals, too. And it's all done for one purpose, and one purpose only: to encourage and strengthen individuals and families through the life-changing message of Jesus Christ.

• • •

For more information about the ministry, or if we can be of help to your family, simply write to Focus on the Family, Colorado Springs, CO 80995 or call (800) A-FAMILY (232-6459). Friends in Canada may write Focus on the Family, PO Box 9800, Stn Terminal, Vancouver, BC V6B 4G3 or call (800) 661-9800. Visit our Web site—www.family.org—to learn more about Focus on the Family or to find out if there is an associate office in your country.

We'd love to hear from you!

Other Faith Strengtheners
From Focus on the Family®

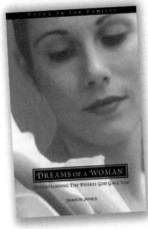

Dreams of a Woman

Girlhood dreams shape almost every woman's life. But what happens when those dreams seem to be on hold—or denied? In *Dreams of a Woman*, author Sharon Jaynes encourages women to reconsider their desires and allow God to surpass their dreams. Includes Bible study questions. Paperback.

Forever in Our Hearts

When miscarriage—or the later death of a baby—shatters hopes and dreams, the loss is accentuated by the fact that few memories or reminders of the child's brief life remain. Therefore, creating a "memory book" can be tremendously healing. *Forever in Our Hearts* is a lovely 24-page album with soft vanilla pages that guides a grieving woman or couple through the process of memorializing a baby. As journal writings, memorabilia and pictures are added, a treasure of peace and strength will emerge. Comfort yourself or a loved one with this tender gift! Hardcover with wire binding.

• • •

Look for these special books in your Christian bookstore or request a copy by calling (800) A-FAMILY (232-6459). Friends in Canada may write Focus on the Family, PO Box 9800, Stn Terminal, Vancouver, BC V6B 4G3 or call (800) 661-9800.

Visit our Web site (www.family.org) to learn more about the ministry or find out if there is a Focus on the Family office in your country.

04/09/24